D0173929

O4A
14

The Path to
PROFITS

AN ENTREPRENEUR'S GUIDE TO **HAVING IT ALL** ... AND STILL **HAVING A LIFE!**

Michelle Jacobik

WORLDCHANGERS
M E D I A

Copyright ©2022 by Michelle Jacobik. All rights reserved.

All rights reserved. No part of this book may be reproduced or used in any manner without the prior written permission of the copyright owner, except for the use of brief quotations in a book review. To request permissions, contact the publisher at publisher@worldchangers.media.

DISCLAIMER: This is a work of nonfiction. Nonetheless, some of the names and identifying character traits of people featured in the stories herein have been changed in order to protect their identities (including stories used with the subject's full permission). Any resulting resemblance to persons either living or dead is entirely coincidental.

The publisher and the author make no representations or warranties of any kind with respect to this book or its contents, and assume no responsibility for errors, inaccuracies, omissions, or any other inconsistencies herein. The content of this book is for entertainment purposes only and is not intended to diagnose, treat, cure, or prevent any condition or disease, including mental health conditions. You understand that this book is not intended as a substitute for consultation with a licensed practitioner. The use of this book implies your acceptance of this disclaimer.

At the time of publication, the URLs displayed in this book refer to existing websites owned by the author and/or the author's affiliates. WorldChangers Media is not responsible for, nor should be deemed to endorse or recommend, these websites; nor is it responsible for any website content other than its own, or any content available on the internet not created by WorldChangers Media.

Hardcover: 978-1-955811-28-6
Paperback: 978-0-578-32157-8
E-book: 978-1-955811-06-4
LCCN: 2022912802

First hardcover edition: September 2022

Cover photo by Pure Fotografica
Design & Typesetting by Bryna Haynes

Published by WorldChangers Media
PO Box 83, Foster, RI 02825
www.WorldChangers.Media

Dedication

This book is dedicated to my mother, Rosemarie Kalin, and my maternal grandmother, Emilia Lavallee, whose examples of compassion, kindness, faith, courage, and humility were the soil in which I planted my own seeds in life. I love you.

Praise

"I murder people for a living. Before that I was an Internet entrepreneur. Before that I wrote for film and TV. Before that I was an advertising executive. My point: I've learned enough about shifting gears and goals to recognize great career and business advice when I see it. Michelle Jacobik's *The Path To Profits* will not only change your perspective, it just might change your life."

Marshall Karp, *New York Times* #1 bestselling author of The NYPD RED series, and The Lomax and Biggs Mysteries

"As entrepreneurs we often start a business because we want something 'more'—more freedom, more flexibility, or more money. But seldom do we experience these things because we get bogged down in the day-to-day of running our business. And when that happens, we're left questioning, 'Why do we do this?' Not anymore. Michelle changes all that by providing the exact blueprint to growing a business—and life—that you will truly love."

Stu McLaren, cofounder of Searchie.io and The Membership Experience™

"Whether you're chasing one dream after another like a squirrel, or mapping out the future of your business without aligning your vision and values, Michelle holds your hand every step of the way—helping you reassess the big picture so you can reach your goals. Her practical advice, honesty about her own struggles, and easy-to-follow revenue mapping and path to profitability strategies make this a must-read for any entrepreneur who wants to make money and have a life while doing it."

Jessica Abo, award-winning journalist, contributor to Entrepreneur.com, sought-after media trainer, and author of *Unfiltered: How to Be As Happy As You Look On Social Media*

"One of the most important things I look for when deciding whom I will learn from to apply their advice is knowing that the 'teacher' has integrated successfully what they are teaching. Michelle Jacobik practices in her own life everything she teaches in this book, *The Path To Profits*. If you are ready to step off the 'check-to-check' treadmill and design the life of your dreams, then this is a must-read. As if holding your hand, Michelle will inspire and guide you to look at your numbers from an empowered place, and encourage you to embrace a profitable and prosperous life of intentionality and design."

Sandra Yancey, CEO and founder of eWomenNetwork

"In *The Paths To Profits*, financial genius Michelle Jacobik lays out a wonderfully architected journey for entrepreneurs to make more money while living their most joyous life. It's the exact roadmap every entrepreneur is seeking but, more importantly, *needs!* The level of care, relatability, and clarity this read provides is valuable and rare. It's a must-read!"

Shannon Crotty, founder and CEO of Polka Dot Powerhouse

"As our world evolves into a more light-filled, conscious planet, and as humans evolve into more loving, healed, spiritually-connected versions of themselves, we need tools to guide us in developing businesses that are not only profitable, but deeply fulfilling. *The Path to Profits* is the perfect tool to help entrepreneurs create businesses that support them in every aspect of their lives—financially, of course—but also in living balanced, healthy, and heart-centered lives. *The Path to Profits* is a must for all entrepreneurs to clarify their vision and create an ever-expanding dream of more profits, freedom, balance, and fun."

Boni Lonnsburry, author of the award-winning books,
The Map* and *The Map to Abundance

"Michelle is raw and real and proof of what she speaks about. She is a true entrepreneur who has reached a rare level of success and managed to integrate all the necessary elements required for a great recipe for life. What Michelle shares in her book is a brilliant reminder of why we become entrepreneurs: *Freedom!* And in order to achieve that status, it takes strategic steps that go beyond the normal operations of a business to achieve scalability, so Michelle gives you her practical, proven advice on how to do this. I loved the simplicity in which she provided key data to running a business, so no matter where you are in your entrepreneurial journey, you'll be able to understand and apply what you need to do."

Tracy Repchuk, 9x bestselling author, speaker, entrepreneur

"Wow, is this good! If you are looking for a clear path to profit, you just found it … all laid out in black and white. It doesn't get better than this!"

Kym Yancey, president and CMO of eWomen Network

"In her new book, *The Path To Profits*, financial expert and author Michelle Jacobik shares a potent personal journey of discovering how embracing the challenges of owning a business can actually become a gift. She details a natural way you can embrace the 'stuckness' and 'cash flow fog,' and then turns on the high beams and sets the path forward, showing you the way to navigate towards your own Path to Profits. This is a must-read book for any Entreprenista."

Stephanie Cartin, cofounder of Entreprenista

"Michelle captivates you in her new book, sharing stories of her own experiences as well as that of others who have stepped on her EnVision success path, so you know you are not alone on this entrepreneurial journey. Her 'Path to Profits' is a proven system to live by, and it keeps you on track as a business owner to create the life and business you want. Commit to *The Path to Profits* and you will have the compounded effect of your efforts in all areas of your life!"

Jen Jones, CEO Jones & Jones Realty, author of the Amazon bestseller, *INTRO-PRENEUR*, and founder of Connect & Elevate

"You can't get on the road to living the life you want without a map and directions. Michelle's EnVision process is the navigation system you need to get clear on what you want so your work drives the life you truly want and deserve. You can work in alignment with passion and purpose while making substantial profits; the key is having the right people and processes in place to guide you. Michelle, thank you for creating a new paradigm to help great leaders have transformational breakthroughs!"

Lorrie Thomas Ross, The Marketing Therapist®
CEO of Web Marketing Therapy®

"In *The Path to Profits*, Michelle Jacobik vividly describes how she came to the decision to make changes in her life, and explains her EnVision framework for successfully balancing life and work. She compellingly encourages readers to take stock and do the work guided by the EnVision roadmap, expanding on each step of the journey and the thought processes and key points of focus, from the identification and clarification of one's values, and then using those to inform one's life vision for the future. She cites clients' experiences with her program to vividly illustrate steps of the progression that have led to more successful and rewarding business and personal lives. Ms. Jacobik is an engaging and enthusiastic author. *The Path to Profits* is hard to put down."

Greg Bonenberger, attorney

"Michelle brings passion and real-life impact to her messages. *The Path To Profits* is a great collection of the best ways to define your financial freedom and live a life of purpose."

Jamie Hopkins, CFP®, managing partner of Wealth Solutions at Carson Group and a Finance Professor of Practice at Creighton University Heider College of Business

"In *The Path to Profits*, Michelle Jacobik shows you how to create a successful business alongside the personal life you aspire to have. In readable, relatable language, Michelle gives nuts-and-bolts tools to create true balance, to live your dreams, and have a thriving business at the same time. Michelle is nonjudgmental and inspiring in her storytelling, encouragement, and guidance, and is the living, breathing proof that her approach works."

Stacy Francis, CFP®, CDFA®, CES™, Savvy Ladies, founder and board chair, Francis Financial, president and CEO, CNBC Financial Advisor Council

Contents

Introduction   1

PILLAR I: VISION

Chapter 1: Is Your Business Running You?   11

Chapter 2: Dream the Dream   23

Chapter 3: Dreams with Deadlines   45

Chapter 4: Evolving the Vision   65

PILLAR II: FLOW

Chapter 5: Getting Real   85

Chapter 6: Level Up to the Dream   107

Chapter 7: Guideposts   121

PILLAR III: GROW

Chapter 8: Growing Your Wings   143

Chapter 9: Your Path to Profits   163

Afterword   173

Resources   177

Acknowledgments   179

About the Author   181

About the Publisher   183

Introduction

_____

WITH MY HEART RACING and my sweaty palms slipping on the steering wheel, I pulled into the parking lot of the radio station to greet the hosts of what would be my first-ever live radio interview.

I was familiar with the inner workings of this radio station—in particular, with its sound booth, as for years radio had been the way I connected with our local market on behalf of the insurance agency I co-owned. I'd spent hours here recording jingles and quick thirty- and sixty-second commercial spots to catch the interest of the "drive-time" listeners. _"You've got to go, go where the savings are / You don't have to go far, just go where the experts are!"_ I'd perfected the timing to the point where I could mention our phone number three times before we cued back to our upbeat outro.

But today was different. I'd been invited here to talk about my new venture—my first offer since retiring from the insurance business—which, at the time, I was calling Sick of the Hustle Coaching.

"Michelle," Steven, one of the hosts of the radio program I was about to appear on, called to me as he climbed out of his own car. "You're not nervous, are you?"

I reached into the passenger seat for my purse and the two copies of Dave Ramsey's *Total Money Makeover* I'd brought as gifts. I fumbled, and everything spilled to the ground. Yes, I was nervous—but I screwed my game face on and handed my hosts the books and a copy of my suggested talking points for our interview. I'd spent all morning running through these, preparing for my fifteen minutes on air.

Steven laughed out loud. "We won't be needing those! We talked on the way over and we know exactly where we want to go today."

Dean, the other host, had arrived while we were talking. He pulled a piece of paper the size of a napkin out of his pocket. A few notes were scribbled on it. "We know you want to help people get out of debt, save money, and build wealth. We're going to lead with this"—he handed me the paper—"and see where we go."

"This" turned out to be a leading statistic. Turns out, real estate professionals rank in the top ten on the suicide statistic list, just under physicians and financial advisors.

"Suicide?" I squeaked. "We are *not* going to lead with suicide!"

"Yes, we are. This shit is real. And this does not have to

be the culmination of people's lives. We want our industry to thrive, not die." Steven and Dean were both Realtors. This was personal to them.

Steven smiled. "Come on, let's have some fun."

Fun? This was going to be a freaking disaster!

In that moment, I knew I had a choice: I could leave, or I could stay. I could argue, or I could accept that despite my careful preparation, I was still going to be winging it on live radio. We were going on air in eight minutes, so I didn't have much time to deliberate—but in the end, it really wasn't a hard choice. I'd come here to do this, so I would. After all, I reasoned, the show *was* called "Straight UP"—and this was going to be just about as straight as it got.

"Okay," I said at last. "Let's do this."

We went inside and settled into the booth. The more I stared at the microphone, the more my stomach jumped.

"One minute left," the producer said into our headphones.

Dean asked, "How can listeners reach you these days?"

"Sick of the hustle dot com."

He laughed. "Really? Why?"

"It's personal," I replied.

You see, everyone in our area was curious as to why I'd left the insurance field—why I'd retired when I was still so young and seemed to love it so much. Why, as a well-respected expert in that field, I'd walked away with no plans to come back. People wondered: was there a *story*?

Well, there was a story, even if it wasn't the one they expected. I left because I was sick of the hustle—and that truth seemed like a perfect name for my business in this chapter of life. I had a deep desire to do things differently.

Dean laughed. "Michelle, I call bullshit on that. You don't know how to not hustle. You love business. You're passionate about all that you do, and I can't see this being any different. Hustle is your middle name. It's in your blood."

That wasn't the compliment he thought it was.

You see, I might not have expected the statistics on real estate agents, but I knew the stats around insurance all too well. The number one cause of death for insurance agency owners was heart attacks. The average age of death? Fifty. I'd spent twenty-six years hustling in that industry and had just turned forty-five. Not long before my retirement I'd landed in the emergency room with what I thought was a heart attack, but what was actually severe anxiety. Other health issues had been creeping in. If I had kept going, my business might have killed me. I knew it.

It seemed real estate was no different. It was an industry that came with significant earning potential, but also significant risk—and risk is stressful.

Dean's comment hit home because I didn't *want* to hustle anymore. Even if hustle was in my blood, it was no longer serving me. I wanted to do less and live more.

And so, we opened the interview with suicide.

That day, I became even more passionate about helping business owners set their financial foundations, make more money, and live their dreams. My fifteen-minute spot turned into thirty; the other guest got stuck in traffic, and Dean and Steven invited me to stay on because our conversation was so synergistic.

Today, my business looks very different from "sick of the hustle dot com." However, my "why" is still intact: my mission is to show entrepreneurs and business owners everywhere that there is a better way. As a success coach and profitability expert for entrepreneurs, I've helped thousands of people to stop sacrificing their lives on the altars of their businesses, find clarity around their ideal lives and work, and change the way they relate to money, work, and success.

Before I left the insurance industry, I was walking a dark road. Actually, I was running it like a marathon. All of my metrics for success were tied to money and power—not power as in "build a mega-corporation to take over the world," but power as in "get to and stay in the top 1 percent in my field." I loved igniting and sustaining customer growth, employee satisfaction and retention, carrier relationships, and especially profit margins. I measured my success and satisfaction by those numbers.

But along the way, I forgot something very important: why I had gone into business in the first place.

When I purchased that business at the age of twenty-nine, I had a vision. I wanted *freedom*. Freedom of time. Freedom of money. Freedom to do whatever the heck I wanted, when I wanted. Over the next fifteen years, I created abundant money freedom, but I somehow forgot that I could have the rest, too. I became so immersed in the metrics of my business that I worked myself sick—literally—and the harder I worked, the darker the road became.

Eventually, I had to stop running and find a new path. That shift—which I'll share much more about throughout this book—was what led me to create the EnVision process, a dynamic new way to align passion, purpose, and profit to support the joy, freedom, and abundance we all desire.

A New Path to Profits

As entrepreneurs, we make thousands of decisions every day. We have choices—so many choices. Sometimes, we forget that one of them is the life we want to live.

There are hundreds—maybe thousands—of great books out there that can tell you how to turn a profit in any type of business. And, the truth is, almost anyone can be profitable if they hustle. In fact, that's how most entrepreneurs I meet operate. They do whatever it takes to succeed in the moment, and everything else—family, relationships, sleep, health, self-care, etc.—gets put on the back burner. For nearly twenty-six years, I did exactly that.

But here's the thing no one tells you. You can be profitable at the expense of your life ... or you can be profitable in support of it. It takes a different approach to create success that supports life, but it's a choice you can make for yourself right now. Today. In this moment.

EnVision is your path to sustainable, nourishing, *aligned* profitability.

In this book, you'll learn how to create a vision that will lead you out of the dark and into a life you don't need a vacation from. More, you'll learn exactly what actions to take to create the profits and cash flow pathways that support that vision.

It's heart-wrenching to see passionate people with dreams of entrepreneurship implode because they've lost their way inside the hustle. To see them failing to make their mark on the world with their unique gifts and talents because they're too busy being busy. To see them failing to bring their beautiful dreams and aspirations to fruition. To see them failing to create and claim the prosperity they desire and the abundance they deserve.

The statistics are clear: more than 65 percent of businesses fail in their first ten years. This doesn't happen because their founders lack purpose or passion. More often than not, it's because they lack clarity and education around the day-to-day realities of business.

In order to thrive, every business needs a road map and a runway. We need to know where we're going. We need a system to help us move toward our goals while still leaving room to pivot when we hit a roadblock. And we need support and guidance in place to help us build momentum before we can soar.

It is absolutely possible for you to make and keep money in your life without working yourself to death. It is absolutely possible to step off the dark road and onto a path where your next steps are clear. But if you want that kind of freedom, clarity, and alignment, you have to be willing to step back from the metrics, measurements, and benchmarks, and ask that all-important question: "What do I actually want out of my life?"

Yes, you actually get to ask that question.

By the time you finish this book, it's my intention that you will not only fully EnVision the life and business of your dreams, but also gain a solid financial footing so that you can flip the statistic and build a new, positive, life-affirming model for business success. All I ask is that you keep an open mind and be willing to see new and better possibilities for your life and business.

So whether you're dreaming of hosting retreats by the beach in Naples, Florida, building a sustainable work community in your hometown, changing the world through product innovation, or something else entirely, buckle up, baby. It's time to get started.

PILLAR I
Vision

CHAPTER 1

Is Your Business Running You?

***

I'LL NEVER FORGET the day I realized that I wasn't running my successful million-dollar business. Instead, it was running me.

I had booked a much-needed vacation with my family in Saint Petersburg, Florida. On our way to the airport, everyone was so excited. "I can't believe we get you to ourselves for a whole week!" my son told me. I could hardly believe it either—but I was excited to get away from the daily grind and spend some meaningful time with my husband and two kids.

My business partner and team of ten dedicated women were prepared to deal with whatever came up while I was away. Although I hadn't asked, they had promised not to call me unless there was a true emergency. "Go enjoy yourself," said Leah, my assistant. "You deserve it."

I did deserve it. When my partner and I purchased the insurance agency over a decade before, it was generating about $600,000 a year in sales. Now, our annual sales were in excess of $12 million. I loved my business, my team, and my clients. I was super proud of what we'd built. We were a pillar of our rural Connecticut community.

But *damn*, did I need a vacation.

The day started out smoothly. We got to the airport in plenty of time. The flight was smooth, and the kids were on their best behavior. We picked up our luggage, piled into a taxi, and set off for the hotel.

Ten minutes into the half-hour taxi ride, my phone rang. It was Leah, calling from the office.

"This had better be good," I muttered. But my heart was sinking. My team wouldn't break their promise not to call unless shit had *really* hit the fan.

"So sorry to bother you," Leah said. "But that big new account you wrote? Another agent just took it out from under you. I've done everything I can, but if we're going to salvage this, I need your help."

We began to hash out a plan to save the account. Once we knew where we stood, Leah transferred me to my lead underwriter. Together, we tried to figure out what happened with the account and how I could play CEO hardball to get it back. Meanwhile, my family and I arrived at the hotel and moved through the lobby to the seating area.

Forty-five minutes later, I was still on the phone, pacing the glistening marble floors as I rattled off instructions. I looked at my kids, arms folded and feet swinging as they waited in the lobby chairs, and thought, *They're always waiting for me.*

It felt like I'd been stabbed in the heart.

When I finally wrapped up with Leah (who, once again, promised not to call unless it was vital), I took a deep breath, swallowed my guilty tears, and herded everyone to the check-in desk to begin our vacation.

Part of me was already justifying what had just occurred. *Stuff happens when you own a business. It comes with the territory. If you don't like it, go work for someone else.* And, let's face it: if Leah hadn't called me, I would have been livid.

But another part of me was asking, *Is this really all there is?*

I knew I had issues with overworking. Although I had a fantastic team, I was always in competition with myself to outdo our biggest year, our biggest month. We won all the "top agent" bonuses and trips. My husband at the time was a stay-at-home dad and managed the kids' school and game schedules, so most days I was the first one in the office, and the last to leave—and it had paid off in a big way. That drive came with substantial rewards—but it also came with a lot of pressure.

While other business owners I knew were coaching their kids' games, I barely made it to my kids' first and last games of the season—and sometimes took phone calls from the bleachers. While others reduced their work hours for the summer, I was sitting on three non-profit boards and was halfway through my presidency year on the board of our local Chamber of Commerce. While others pursued passions outside of their businesses, I neglected just about everything that wasn't moving the needle in my company—including my body and health.

How many times? I wondered a few hours later, as I watched my kids splash in the hotel pool. *How many times have I asked my kids, "Please give Mommy five more minutes"? How many times have I said, "I just have to write this email," or, "I just have to make this one phone call"?*

How have my priorities gotten so messed up?

Then, that old, familiar voice spoke up in my head. *You chose to own a business. This is what you signed up for.*

No, said yet another voice—softer, almost a whisper. *It doesn't have to be this way.*

EnVision Your Best Life

It took me several years and many burnt bridges after that day in the hotel before I finally got off the hamster wheel of over-working, stopped burning the candle at both ends, and began to dream again.

When I did that, everything changed.

In 2009, I separated from my husband. While we were amazing co-parents, we weren't good partners anymore. I had just been too wrapped up in my work to realize that our marriage wasn't serving either of us. However, because of the financial pressures inherent to the divorce, I went right back to overworking. *I can't let things slip now!* I reasoned.

However, that created even more pressure in my family life. My former husband and I had shared custody, which meant we switched off with the kids every two days. Having relied on him to hold the fort at home for so long, I had no idea how to navigate my kids' schedules and needs along with everything

I was already doing. I desperately wanted to spend more time with them; they needed me, and I needed them. But if I didn't do my part at work, we'd all be in trouble.

By 2013, I was financially stable again but felt totally burned out. With the help of a life coach, I started asking questions like, "What is most important to me?" and "What does my ideal day look like?"

Just a few weeks into this process, I knew the time had come. I needed to step away from my business so I could step into my life.

That moment of decision came *eight years* after the incident in the hotel. Eight more years in the storm. Eight more years of overworking, overachieving, and missing out on life. There were *so many more times* in those eight years when life called me to show up and prioritize the things that were most import-ant—but I didn't know how to do it. I didn't know how to make the decisions that would lead me to better experiences. I didn't know what questions to ask, or what help to seek out. But once I finally saw the path to change, I stepped onto it with both feet. Mere months (and a major inner shift) after those initial coaching sessions, I sold my share of the insurance business and totally redesigned my life.

For the first time ever, I felt like I could just ... be.

And that feeling changed *everything*.

So many entrepreneurs I know are *exactly* where I was that day in the hotel: overworked, overconnected, and overdoing everything. Maybe that's where you are, too. Maybe you started your business to create freedom but ended up shackled to a time-eating monster that never gives you a break. Maybe that monster is making you money—or maybe it's eating every last dime.

Through sleep-deprived eyes, you might see slick Facebook ads promising "$10k a day from one sales page!" or "Manifest money instantly using this meditation technique!" Scrolling through your feed, you might feel a sense of guilt and shame wash over you, and wonder, *Why is this so easy for everyone else, but so hard for me?*

You're likely exhausted. Struggling. Throwing money and solutions around in the hopes that something will stick. Carrying "investments" that once felt like opportunities but are now just debt. Guilty. Ashamed. Lacking confidence. Wondering if you are even on the right path.

Or, maybe you've reached a place where you're successful and making great money, but the stuff that was once so enticing now feels empty. The house, the cars, the clothes … they're no longer enough to justify burning the candle at both ends. You want to live a life of meaning and do your part to make the world a better place, but you lack clarity about where or how to begin.

No matter what your current situation, my guess is that you picked up this book because you still dream of a day when your business exists to empower, support, and impact you and your clients in a meaningful, balanced way—and because part of you is terrified that, if you don't change something soon, that day might never come.

The Bureau of Labor Statistics has shared that more than half of new businesses fail in the first twelve months. Approximately 20 percent of businesses fail by year two, 45 percent by year five, and 65 percent by year ten. Only *25 percent* of new businesses make it beyond fifteen years of life.

Some of those failures occur because of logistics, market variations, or even natural disasters. But the vast majority occur because business owners don't have the right visioning, planning, and management tools. Or, the difference between the founders' dreams for the business and the actual reality of running it are simply too far apart from one another to be sustainable. Without a clear vision, tools to create flow, and a plan to grow, things can quickly spin out of control.

I'm here to tell you that there *is* a way out of the entrepreneurial spiral. You can have freedom of money, time, *and* action in your business. You can make an impact and still have a life. But if you really want it all—the freedom *and* the success, the money *and* the time—you need to be willing to challenge everything you thought you knew about designing, building, and running a business.

The EnVision process is your ticket to having it all.

How to Use This Book

In this book, I'll share with you the three pillars of the EnVision framework I developed to transform my own relationship with life and work while, at the same time, designing a profitable, scalable business model that creates life-changing results for my clients. This is the same process I teach at my sold-out live and virtual EnVision events and use with my private clients. In fact, using exactly what you're about to learn in this book, I've helped thousands of entrepreneurs stop overworking and underearning, and start living the lives they've always imagined.

Here's a snapshot of what's in store for you:

In Pillar I—*Vision*—you'll discover why a "business model" should always and only be built on a "life model." I'll show you how to create a holistic, encompassing vision that can be easily translated into actionable goals, instead of living a half-life in the ether of "someday."

In Pillar II—*Flow*—we'll bring your vision to life in a tangible way through the numbers. In particular, we'll look at what your dream life actually costs, and design a business plan and personal budget to support it. (This is totally contrary to what most of us were taught!)

And finally, in Pillar III—*Grow*—we'll set up action steps to help you grow into your dream life and business. We'll put a spotlight on your business through aligned marketing and visibility. You'll understand exactly how to crush your new, audacious goals—and, eventually, expand beyond them—all while working less, enjoying your life more, and feeling fully on purpose and aligned with your vision.

But all of this comes with one caveat—

You must do the work.

The people who are most successful—and yes, this includes people who are successful at designing their dream lives, following their passions, and working less while earning more—are those who understand that, in order to get the most out of any system or process, you need to engage with it fully. In the context of this book, this means doing the exercises, following the journaling prompts, taking action on the goals you set, and giving 100 percent of your attention to the creation of your vision.

Will you benefit from simply reading this book and cognitively understanding your Path to Profits? Absolutely. Once you learn something, you can never un-learn it. But life-changing results don't come from theory. They come from action—specifically, from actions that are aligned with a strong vision.

The Gift of Stuckness

Chances are, you picked up this book because you're feeling stuck in some way—like you're not moving forward, like you're not moving fast enough, or like you're stuck on a treadmill with the speed turned up to ten.

Before we get into the work of creating your Path to Profits, I want you to understand that being stuck is a gift.

If we don't understand or aren't clear about what is going on in our lives and businesses, there is no way to find a solution. So, "stuck" is actually a great place to be. The discomfort of stuckness—of not accomplishing what we have decided to do, not being the best version of ourselves, or not living our best life—forces us to slow down, get clear, and finally do something about it.

Most of us don't look at stuckness this way. Instead, we worry. We complain. We numb ourselves with wine, or drugs, or Netflix. We put on a brave face and keep grinding away, but inside we're asking, "Is this really all there is?"

The truth is, there *is* more for you. It's there—in the dreams you journal about, in your biggest goals, in your fondest wishes.

Those things are your higher self showing you *what is possible*, because it knows what you really want out of life and how best to get there. Chances are, it was your higher self that whispered, "Come on, let's start this business. Let's go meet some new people and chase these big ideas of yours. Let's go on an adventure!" And you listened!

Yet, on the other hand, you have your human self—your ego, and its natural desire to protect you from harm, discomfort, and the unknown at any cost. Your higher self and ego are always circling one another, vying for your attention, because everything that you want but don't yet have falls into the category of "uncertain and unknown."

The EnVision process alleviates stuckness because it gives both your higher self and your human self what they want and need. The higher self gets to create a totally awesome vision, complete with all the bells and whistles, while the human self gets the certainty and comfort of clear goals, hard numbers, and measurable successes.

The people who truly succeed as entrepreneurs—who create the dream life *and* the dream business—aren't superhuman. They have simply figured out how to get their higher self and their human self moving in the same direction.

You are capable of doing whatever you dream. And the part of you who dreams knows it.

I won't lie: doing this work will likely bring up a lot of stuff for you. Challenging emotions. Self-doubt. Fears. Things you'd rather avoid.

I want you to know that it's all okay. There's no such thing as perfect (whatever your ego might say). Therefore, I'm not going to ask that you do this work perfectly. I'm simply going to ask that you do it with *presence*.

Give yourself the gift of full presence with your vision: your dream, goals, fears, higher self, and human self. Pay attention to what comes up, rather than sidestepping or squashing it because you're too busy. Love your future enough to make space in your present to create it.

Why?

Because in the end, your Path to Profits isn't just about money. It's about being who you came here to be: a passionate, purposeful human who is helping other humans in a tangible way. More, it's about living as you were ultimately designed by your higher power to live—as the fullest, most joyful, most abundant version of you.

CHAPTER 2

Dream the Dream

EVERY YEAR ON JANUARY 1, I create my vision for the year and identify the things I want to accomplish. I've been making three-year vision boards since I was twenty, and I've always known that I have the power to create whatever I can imagine.

On January 1, 2014, just weeks after finalizing the sale of my insurance business, I gathered my tools and sat down to create my new board.

I was looking at a blank slate. My canvas was empty. My calendar was empty.

I was finally, totally, and completely *free*.

And I had no idea what the hell to *do* with this freedom. Who was I without the title, the accolades, the victories, and the constant hustle? It was like a huge piece of my identity had been wiped away. And yet, "freedom" had been on my vision board for decades.

I was blessed to have a substantial cushion from the sale of the business, so there was no need for me to rush into anything new. I had no big goals, no driving deadlines. No strategies to plan. No clients or colleagues to please.

And so, I did something that had never felt possible before.

I started to design a *life*.

As a natural workaholic and performance junkie, I told myself (and others) that I would take twelve weeks off to start my year so I could lean in and figure out what my next chapter would be. To be honest, twelve weeks seemed like a decade. What would I do with all that *time*? But I also knew that truly resetting my priorities would take some breathing room. I wanted to make motherhood something that didn't get squeezed in around other tasks, or passed to someone else in the village I'd created to support my kids. I wanted to make self-care and wellness more a priority for myself. But most of all, I wanted to get quiet enough to hear guidance around my next steps from the divine and my inner self.

Around week eleven, my phone started ringing. My inbox exploded. "What is happening?" people were asking. "What are you going to do?"

My first thought was, *Why do they care?* But I soon realized that my resistance wasn't caused by others' curiosity, but because I still didn't have an answer for them—or for me. So, I started replying, "I've decided to take the whole year off."

And so began what I now refer to as my Freedom Year.

I leaned into freedom. Real freedom—not the "freedom" of owning a business but also working eighty-plus hours a week. I created fun in every day, not just on vacation days. I learned to relax, and to breathe again. Best of all, I started finding balance in my life for the first time.

Also for the first time, what went on my vision board was bigger and more powerful than just "stuff." For years, I'd identified the next big vacation destination, the next glamorous purchase, the next luxury car—and I'd created everything on my board, year after year. But all of that stuff was empty, because I wasn't happy or fulfilled. I'd created the things but forgotten the feelings.

Now, I filled my vision board with words. Words that represented feelings. Words that represented what life and living meant to me. Words that inspired the feelings I wanted to live into, rather than the things I wanted to buy or achieve. My vision board became a guide for how I wanted my life to evolve, versus how I wanted to gather things and experiences. This new approach helped me to finally tune into and be with what I truly wanted—the grandeur of life as an experienced whole. And that changed everything.

After a year of exploring life, I knew it was time to create something new on the business side. However, I had no idea what that could be. I wanted a business I could run from any-where—travel and adventure are non-negotiables for me—but I also wanted to do something purposeful. I wanted a model that could eventually generate passive income, and that would allow me the flexibility I needed so I could continue to priori-tize my personal life and family.

In early 2015, I started asking myself, "How do I want my life to look and feel—and how can I build a business model around *that*?"

I started to explore the things I had loved about my former work in the insurance world. The answers? Advising and educating people around their choices. Helping people take concrete steps toward their big dreams. Building meaningful relationships. Being a loving leader.

How could I do those things while still enjoying the new, more balanced life that had opened up for me?

The answer was clear: take my decades of accumulated knowledge and become a speaker, consultant, strategic advisor, and strategist.

My business has gone through many iterations since that time (I'll share more about that process in Chapter 3), but the core of the vision is still the same: create a vibrant, abundant, inspiring life that I love, and empower others to do the same.

This is the power of vision.

Vision is Everything

When I first met Leslie, she'd been an entrepreneur for more than two decades, and had started multiple businesses in diverse sectors including retail, events, coaching, and food service. The problem was that none of them had lasted. Most hadn't come close to being profitable. She had a great work ethic and good ideas, but just couldn't seem to get any of her endeavors off the ground.

"I've had a twenty-year losing streak," she told me. "I feel like a total failure."

"You're not a failure," I told her. "You just haven't been operating from a clear vision."

Like many creative entrepreneurs, Leslie struggled with "squirrel syndrome." She loved to chase the next big idea. Each time she started a new venture, she dove in headfirst with a huge amount of purpose and passion, but soon got distracted and frustrated because things weren't unfolding as quickly as she wished. She had a vision for financial freedom, but no long-term plan to get there other than "make lots of money, fast." So, when her latest venture wasn't generating income at the rate she desired, she would scrap it and start something new. It was a cycle of reactionary behavior that wasn't helping her create the business and life she really wanted.

Despite the challenges, however, her ideas were solid. In my opinion, most of her past businesses could have been successful if she'd created a clear vision and given herself a long enough runway to focus on the steps to profitability.

In our work together, we uncovered that Leslie had a true gift for empowering and connecting people. (She'd even written a book about it!) She decided that it was time to leverage that gift in the form of a virtual assistance agency. Excited, she was ready to jump right in and design a business plan, but she stopped herself short.

"I'm so afraid that if I do this, if I go all in, it will end up like all of my other businesses," she confided. "The last thing I need is another wish that doesn't come true."

"You're right," I answered. "We need to do this differently."

The thing about chasing dreams is that, most of the time, we don't have a solid plan for what happens *after* our dreams come true. We're wandering in the fog, chasing the faint glow of the sun behind the clouds. Too often, the chasing becomes the whole story.

Over the course of her previous twenty years of entrepreneurial ups and downs, the one thing Leslie *didn't* do was actually map out what she wanted from her life, and then set clear parameters for how she wanted her business to support that vision. She simply pointed herself in a direction, got to work, and hoped for the best. Sure, she had basic monetary goals for each of her businesses, but her "on the fly" approach consistently failed to produce the results she wanted.

I've seen wishing and waiting turn too many entrepreneurs onto the dark roads of financial strain, burnout, and despair. They've invested everything in the belief that they will get there … and yet, they still have no real idea where "there" is. They just know it's better, and different, than here.

To me, this is a huge reason why entrepreneurial failure is rampant. Most entrepreneurs don't lack talent, heart, or even business sense. They simply don't know how to turn their wishes into plans, and their plans into profits.

Since you picked up this book, I'd be willing to guess that this rings true for you at some level. Maybe, like Leslie, your ideal life is leagues ahead (financially and otherwise) of where your current profits stand, and you have a hard time even imagining how you will bridge that chasm. Or maybe you're where I was ten years ago—creating real profit, but with no life to show for it. These may seem like two separate challenges, but they're really just two sides of the same coin. Both situations occur when we don't create, and execute on, a clear and powerful vision.

A clear vision for your life, combined with a planned path to profitability, will make a lot of common entrepreneurial problems evaporate.

Vision helps you manage squirrel syndrome as well as workaholism. It helps you seize opportunities even when you don't feel ready. It can help you get ahead of trends, secure funding, and create a "blue ocean" space beyond competition and scarcity.

But most importantly, vision will keep you in an aligned space where you can make sound decisions. When you have a clear path forward, you are more likely to invest your time, energy, and money into the *right* things at the *right* times. That doesn't mean that you won't have moments of uncertainty—only that you'll be clearly able to identify when an investment or opportunity is wrong for you (or when it's the right thing at the wrong time). We'll talk more about this in Chapter 3; for now, just know that discernment and vision go hand in hand.

When I asked Leslie what her ideal life looked like, she honestly had no idea how to answer. Like most people, she had some vague ideas about her "dream life"—nice house, nice car, swimming pool, college tuitions managed, etc.—but she hadn't really considered the details beyond that. "I figured I'd sort that part out when I had actual profits to work with," she confessed.

I knew that swirl well. For years, I'd spent my time and energy reacting to the needs of my business. I went where the latest business goal (or crisis) pointed me. I had a (very cloudy) idea about what a "better life" would look like, but no clue how to get there. I was great about taking vacations, but there was no balance when I was back on the ground. I figured someday I'd have the time to do all the things I wanted to do—for myself, for my family, and for my community—but that time was, quite clearly, not now.

This approach is absolutely backward. How can you work toward what you want if you don't even know what that is? How can you expect your business to make room for your life when you don't have clear boundaries and expectations in place?

That's why, in this chapter, I'm going to walk you through the process for creating a clear vision—not for your business, but for your *life*. In fact, we're going to evaluate your dreams for every part of your life, and get super clear on what you actually want your life to look like on a day-to-day basis. This will set a baseline for how much income you want/need to support your ideal lifestyle, what income streams you create through your business, how you structure your time, and what you do (and don't) need to pay attention to.

With this knowledge in hand, you will be able to set powerful goals and boundaries in your business to support the lifestyle and freedom you want and deserve. You will truly be empowered to create your dream life—not in just one area, but in every area: career, physical health, emotional well-being, spirituality/personal growth, family, social/community relationships, and finances.

Yes, I'm going to show you how to design a vision that helps it all work together!

But first, let me ask you …

WHAT DO YOU WANT?

"What Do I *Want*?"

This is the most important question you can ask when designing your vision.

The question sounds simple, but it's often difficult to answer. Allowing yourself to explore your deepest desires can be frightening. Maybe you think you don't have the time to consider something as "fanciful" as what you actually want out of your life. Or maybe you think it's too late to accomplish all the things you dream about. But a fulfilling life—like a successful business—doesn't happen by accident. It happens by design.

In this chapter, we're going to begin the deep, transformational process of uncovering your vision. This work will ask you to consider every aspect of your life—personal and professional, tangible and intangible. So, as we dive into the first building blocks of vision—namely, your core values and your personal "why"—give yourself permission to dream. Think about what you want, not what you don't want. Dig a little deeper than you've allowed yourself to do before. Consider the dreams you never thought were possible. Most of all, lean into what really matters to you in your life and work.

That crucial question, "What do I want?" can feel selfish and self-centered at first. Many of us were born and bred into religious and cultural belief systems that glorify suffering and selflessness as a means of earning bonus points in the hereafter. Still others of us have life experiences and traumas that have made it feel unsafe to ask for what we want. If you have fears or limitations in these areas (or any others), it will be important for you to seek aligned and professional support to work through these conditioned responses. When you begin to heal these wounds, you will be able to tap into your vision in a truly expanded way.

Whatever your starting point, creating your vision will require time, reflection, and patience. Your most powerful vision will bloom from your biggest and most joyful hopes, dreams, and aspirations. It will resonate with your core values and fuel your "why." And, with planning, it will help you take the seeds of your desires from planting to harvest.

FEELINGS, NOT THINGS

To me, "vision" is the big picture of how I want to *feel* in my life. It's a deeper consciousness—one that we begin to walk with when we start asking ourselves the right questions. It's a way of aligning with what we want, and what Soul and our higher power want for us.

As I shared earlier, for years my vision revolved around things: The latest luxury car, the five-star resort in the Swiss Alps. To me, those represented freedom and adventure—but was I actually choosing those things? When I started to lean into the essence of what I desired, I could see the disconnect. I wanted the feeling *way* more than the stuff, and the stuff wasn't truly creating the feeling.

So were freedom, adventure, and joy—words that had been on my vision board for decades—*actually* priorities for me? Or were they pipe dreams: nice to think about, but not actually within reach? Was I willing to do what it took to create these things, or was I just reiterating them because I liked the way they sounded? Questions like these opened up a whole new way of thinking for me.

If you've experienced any form of coaching, personal growth work, or corporate leadership training, you've probably done some form of vision work. The exercises later in this chapter may feel familiar. However, a lot of other methods confuse vision with goals. They tell you to strive for the things, the achievements, the accolades, and the benchmarks, and call those things "vision." But that's not what vision is about.

Goals and vision are different. They're like the two magnifications in progressive eyeglass lenses. When you look down at what's right in front of you—like you would with the "reading" lenses in progressives—you're looking at goals. When you look out at the horizon—the "distance" lenses—you're in vision. But when you try to look at both at once? That's a recipe for blurriness, confusion, and a headache.

Also, when we confuse vision with goals, we're likely to also confuse material success with happiness. We think the stuff, the benchmarks, and the achievements will create the feelings that we want to feel. Nine times out of ten, this doesn't work. It certainly didn't for me. Instead, we need to decide how we want to feel (vision) before we can deliberately and strategically create the things (goals) that support it.

So, as we move into the instructional part of this chapter, remember that there is more to vision than the strategic planning view. You need to lift your gaze and explore a more conscious, holistic space. That doesn't mean that strategy has no place in vision—it definitely does—but it needs to come after the big picture of your life is established.

In other words, decide how you want to feel, and who you want to be. Then, apply strategy to get there.

Vision Starts with Values

Georgia walked into my EnVision event asking one question: "What's next for me?"

She'd been following my reinvention journey for a while and had decided that it was time for her to make a change. She'd been working in the family business for more than half her life—but despite her MBA from a leading university and a personality that could outshine any light in the room, when she took a seat at the table beside her dad and uncle, she was inevitably told to "pipe down and take notes." In fact, she was treated like a glorified secretary—right down to slinging coffee and sandwiches.

She later shared, "I was told that my ideas were useless and that I knew nothing—that it was a waste of time to teach me anything. I wanted to learn the basics of the business and had a ton of questions that needed answering, but my desire to help was treated as an inconvenience."

Her self-esteem was at an all-time low. She spent years barely living, doing only what it took to get by—until, one day, something shifted. "God and the Universe told me loud and clear that this was not where I was supposed to be. It wasn't meant to be this hard."

When she entered the seaside room at EnVision, Georgia had been working on her healing for some time and had come a long way toward restoring her innate sparkle. She had finally said "Enough is enough!" and stepped away from the family business, but she wasn't clear on where she wanted to go next.

When I presented on core values that day, I saw Georgia pause and take a few deep breaths. Then, I saw her lean right in. She had no resistance to the playful exercise, even though I hadn't made it clear yet where this was all going. She brought her whole self to the table as she identified her top ten core values: Confidence, Education, Faith, Happiness, Humor, Love, Respect, Self-Expression, Service, and Unity.

"I value the experiences I've had," she told me later. "But by staying in a situation where I had so little input and influence, I've been compromising every one of those core values for two decades."

Georgia was open. She had been healing. She had acceptance and forgiveness for her father and uncle. And, as she sat with the core values she'd identified as the most important to her, something powerful came through. She became clear she wanted to work with women and girls and help them find their voice.

By identifying her core values, Georgia found her new vision.

The best way to create a vision for your life and business—whether you're starting fresh, starting over, or expanding in a current venture—is to lean into what you value.

Your core values aren't random buzzwords to post on your office wall and forget about. Nor are they lofty dreams to which you aspire but can't truly connect. Your core values are *the energies that guide your life*, and the underlying motivators for all of your choices. When you know and understand them, they become valuable tools to help you shape your vision and goals in a cohesive way that feels exciting, positive, and aligned for you.

This seems obvious once stated; however, most of us don't innately know our core values. We don't understand what's most important to us. Instead, we turn our focus outward to what our society, culture, and the media value. Without undergoing a discovery process, it's actually quite challenging to strip away the "shoulds" and speculations. Knowing and accepting what you *do* value takes inner work and effort.

While the following process is best done with support, you can do it on your own if you apply patience, reflection, self-honesty, and determination. Here's how to get started.

Take out your journal or a notepad. Take a few deep breaths to clear your mind.

Set a timer for five minutes.

From the worksheet below, choose all of the core values that resonate with you, and write them in your journal. If a value that is top of mind to you isn't on the list, don't worry—write it down anyway.

Once you've identified your top values, write a few thoughts about why each value is important to you, and how you would love to express it in your life.

Adventure	Freedom	Independence	Security
Balance	Fulfillment	Integrity	Self-expression
Confidence	Forgiveness	Kindness	Service
Creativity	God	Love	Spirituality
Discipline	Growth	Lifestyle	Strength
Education	Happiness	Marriage	Success
Faith	Health	Peace of mind	Truth
Family	Hope	Power	Unity
Financial Security	Honesty	Progress	Wealth
Friends	Humor	Respect	Wisdom

For example, the word "joy" was on my vision board for years, but I didn't have a clear idea of what "joy" actually looked and felt like. It was there because it felt like it *should* be there—because who in their right mind wouldn't want more joy in their life? When I asked myself, "Does the word 'joy' actually resonate with me?" the answer was a clear "No!" So I asked, "Okay, what is the essence of 'joy' that I feel connected to?" The answer? *Fun!*

Fun was something I could connect to. When I changed my value terminology from "joy" to "fun," I felt much more connected to the feeling.

Your "Why"—and Why It Matters

Your "why" is a purpose, belief, or cause that is the living expression of your values. When you are an entrepreneur, this is also the driving life force of your business.

The most successful businesses and business leaders have a very strong and defined "why." This sense of purpose and direction helps them to align their values with their actions; the result is that they connect more deeply with their customers, enjoy heightened employee engagement and retention, and create aligned and repeatable profit. Profit isn't a driving force, it's a result of the "why"—and that kind of clarity works. In fact, purpose-driven companies outperform their counterparts in stock price by a factor of twelve!

As Simon Sinek famously said, "People don't buy what you do or how you do it. They buy *why* you do it."

Your "why" is your clarified beliefs and core values pointed in a direction. It will motivate you when things get tough, forge a connection with the people you want to serve, and help you find clarity around challenging decisions. To me, results are a consequence of purposeful process.

Since you are at the helm of your business, your personal "why" will also become the "why" for your business. While the expression of your "why" might look different in your business and personal life, the intention and energy will be the same.

Most entrepreneurs I know have built businesses that only partially overlap their core values and personal "why." Like my first business, their companies don't fully reflect their core values. If this feels true to you, the solution is to clarify your personal core values and "why." Only then can you make adjustments in your business to create alignment, flow, and growth.

My "why" today is about facilitating entrepreneurial success. If, in my lifetime, I can make even a small change in the sad statistics around entrepreneurial failure that I shared in Chapter 1, I will consider my life well spent. This work is in perfect congruency with my core values of freedom, adventure, and joy. I believe that our work can and should free us from financial and creative limitations. And I believe that business should serve life and facilitate joy—both for us and those we serve.

HOW TO FIND YOUR "WHY"

Note: Before you begin this exercise, you will want to complete the core values identification exercise earlier in this chapter.

Spend a few moments journaling on one or more of the following questions:

- What gifts and talents do you want to share with the world and why?

- What have you learned in life that you want to pass on to others?

- What legacy do you want to leave?

- What makes you feel totally excited and alive?

- What do you think is your purpose here on Earth?

Now, write a bit about how your top core values align with your "why." For example, maybe you value family and want to leave a legacy. Or, maybe you value happiness and want to share your talents with the world. Explore what this intersection of core values and purpose means to you and see what comes up!

Write Your Vision Statement

Now, it's time for the fun stuff.

Get out your notebook and pen.

Close your eyes and imagine that you are five years in the future. Envision that you are having the *very best possible day* in your life and business. Feel into the essence of this day. Everything you have been dreaming about is happening, right here, right now, just as you've imagined it! Allow yourself to be in the experience for as long as it takes for it to feel clear and present for you.

Open your eyes and begin to write as your future self. Use present tense, "I AM" language, as though what you have envisioned is already true and happening in the here and now.

Here are some prompts to guide you:

- What do you hear, smell, see, taste, and feel over the course of your perfect day?

- What really matters to you? What no longer feels important?

- What's special about you? What qualities do you have that you're really proud of? What are your talents?

- What is your emotional state? How did you feel in your mind, body, and heart?

- What brings you joy and happiness? What would bring you *even more* joy and happiness?

- What in your life are you most excited about? What are your dreams for the upcoming weeks, months, and years? What are your priorities and goals?

- How are you living out your core values and your "why" as this version of you?

Continue to write until you have a clear picture of the visionary "you." Add any details that feel important. Know that this vision is real, and that it is 100 percent possible for you.

I often ask my one-to-one clients to complete this exercise on their own before we meet. They work really hard at crafting their visions, but their creations end up reading like one long, exhausting to-do list. This is not what we're after here. This is a journal entry *written by your future self*. Let it play out like a movie you're watching, with you as the star in the setting you most love.

You can streamline this writing into a one-page "Vision Statement" later if you like, but don't edit out the magic.

Dig deeper. Feel it. Let it show itself to you.

I promise, it will be worth it.

Vision Changes Everything

When I did the exercises in this chapter with my client Leslie, she realized that she lacked clarity in many areas, but most importantly around the intersection of her core values and "why" with her business goals. Much of her "jumping around" came about because the business models she was exploring at the time didn't align with how she wanted to feel in her life. Instead of changing the business to support her life vision and purpose, she simply ditched the business.

The hard truth is that many entrepreneurs don't create the financial success they desire and deserve because they never take the time to explore whether their personal core values and "why" actually work with the business they're pursuing. And so, it's necessary for all of us to ask (and continue asking): "Is the discontent I feel because of my business as an entity, or because I don't feel my business is supporting my core values and vision for my life?"

Leslie and I met virtually over the course of a few months— and by the time we were done, she had clarity galore! She saw how she had been chasing ideas for two decades but hadn't done the work to create a structured business plan or vet her ideas in the marketplace, let alone stop to ask herself, "Is this a business I really want?"

However, as we worked through her vision, a deeper truth emerged that was much more powerful and revealing.

Leslie didn't have a supportive partner. She had been the sole CEO of her household for every one of those twenty years since she launched her first business. In her pre-family years, she had earned a Master's degree in psychology, but when she and her husband had their first child, it was decided that she would give up her career and stay home with the kids. To hold on to a sliver of her identity and independence, she decided to take the leap and build her first business while she was simultaneously growing, birthing, and raising three little humans born only eighteen months apart.

In those early years, rest and sleep were something she longed for but could never find. While she did her best to build a sustainable business, she was juggling a ton of other responsibilities—and for the most part, doing it alone. As the kids got older, her spouse began to pressure her with statements like, "If it's not working, you'd better figure it out or go get a job." She resented this because he'd been benefiting bigtime from her building her businesses at home while caring for the kids, handling all the household chores, and getting hot meals on the table six nights a week. Not to mention that her "business losses" actually proved to be a tax benefit because they offset her husband's high salary.

The core of the issue was that Leslie had no time to dream. She had no time or energy to work herself through the process of creating an aligned, successful, visionary business. So, she leaped into new ideas, most of which fell into the category of, "There's nothing like it in the market, so it needs to exist!"

In the majority of her business explorations, she was trying to invent something brand new. The ideas were sound, but without a strategic plan to back them up, the ideas didn't grow wings. More, she didn't have the time and energy capacity to actually pull off what she envisioned—accomplishing that, she saw as we reviewed her attempts, would have required some major shifts and shakeups in her life plan.

Through her Vision work, Leslie was able to see both the incredible mom and creative she had been and the grounded, successful woman she was becoming. She learned to see her persistence and resilience in a new light, and claim a new, more confident way of being. Now that she had clarity and direction, she was able to enter into a new level of partnership with her husband—who realized, after some tough conversations, that he hadn't been supportive of her efforts in the ways that truly mattered to her.

Today, Leslie has created a stable, profitable virtual assistant agency. Her clients are mom-preneurs who share her core values around flexibility and parenthood, and who want to run their companies while being home and available to their kids. She employs women like her: driven, multi-talented, and with a huge desire to help others. And she finally has the lifestyle, cash flow, and freedom she dreamed of for so long.

Becoming our own boss means more than just sacrifice. It means having clarity around who we are, what we want, and where we are going—and then actually creating it. Yes, there will be sacrifices made as we implement our vision and goals—but they will be the ones we choose, not the ones we feel are forced on us by our business or the world.

Leslie revisits her core values and "why" regularly, both at my annual EnVision Live events and in her own practices. Unlike before, she regularly invests the time and resources to dig deep and get the clarity she needs to make sound decisions. And when, on hard days, she feels like there's *so* much to do and not enough energy to do it, she returns to her core values, sets aside what no longer serves her, and steps even more firmly into her "why."

"It's so much simpler than I used to think," she tells me. "As long as I know what I want, I can create it."

The same is true for you.

CHAPTER 3

Dreams with Deadlines

WHEN ANGELICA, a successful therapist and toxic relationship expert, engaged me to help her build the online side of her business, she had already invested $45,000 of the $50,000 her business earned in 2021 into this venture. She was an amazing student and a passionate, heart-centered provider who truly was looking to serve more people. Yet, despite doing everything "by the book," Angelica wasn't getting any traction. In fact, she was close to giving up.

"I was spending on all the things I was told I 'needed' to create a successful business," she told me. "Coaching, sales trainings, funnel strategies, webinar software, a social media manager, and Facebook ads. I turned the ads off after three months because I wasn't getting a single qualified lead—but by then I had already spent upwards of $2,500!"

What we found when we looked at her business using the EnVision Path to Profits model was that there were huge disconnects between what she desired and what she was actually building.

In our conversations, Angelica revealed that she hated social media and had no desire to run an online community—and yet, here she was with a growing community. And, despite the hires she had made to help her maintain her online presence, she had eighteen people waiting to get into her free group, and the majority of them had been waiting for eight or more weeks for their requests to be accepted. When we reviewed her financials, I discovered that she hadn't been paying herself at all. Instead, there were four people in front of her with their hands out monthly, even though their efforts were resulting in no sales. Clearly, the social media strategy she had been told was a necessity wasn't working!

However, what *was* working was a $29/month listing on the *Psychology Today* website. Not only was it getting her phone ringing with aligned clients, but it also made it easy for her to be seen as a qualified expert in her field. Once new clients did their first breakthrough session with her, it was a natural next step to enroll in her $6,000 program. The clients coming through this pipeline were paying up front, meaning they were supporting Angelica's vision of never taking insurance.

At first, it might seem that the social media management (and subsequent drain on her resources) was Angelica's biggest problem. After all, those hires and massive ad costs had turned what could have been a six-figure inaugural year into an overall $12,000 loss! However, there was an even bigger issue at play.

Angelica's goals—and the actions they initiated—didn't match her core values, her "why," or her vision for her life.

When we got clear about what Angelica really desired, it was obvious that social media was her least aligned revenue strategy. She wanted to work with people one-to-one, not run a community. She wanted to touch individual people deeply, not reach a broad swath of people in a shallower way. She had no desire to be an online motivational guru. All she wanted was to reach the people who needed her most, in a way that wouldn't burn her out. Her core values of service, happiness, balance, and growth had led her to her career, but they weren't being honored in her current business design. Her service was getting watered down, her happiness was being sucked away (along with all her cash flow), and the people in her group weren't benefiting from growth because she was too overwhelmed to serve them deeply.

Once we understood her core values and "why," Angelica and I were able to set goals for her business, but also for her life. We were able to see precisely where and how to create the balance and space she craved for herself, and from there set goals to drive business success without burning her out.

You see, Angelica not only needed to align her business to her big goals, but to her current season of life. As a single mom with primary custody of her preschool-aged daughter, she didn't have endless energy or time to devote to work or self-care. She had a goal of enrolling her daughter in a Montessori school, but that would mean bringing in an extra $1,200 a month to cover tuition expenses. In order to pull this off, she would need to be diligent about her time management and set better boundaries with both herself and her clients. No more wasting time on social media strategies that weren't getting clients!

In our work together, we looked at what it would actually

take for her to work in her business and on her business, fill her own cup with strategic "recharge" breaks, and still have time to be present for her daughter. At first, she believed these goals were in conflict with one another. How could she bring in an extra $1,200 a month and still have time for everything else? However, by putting her LifeStyle Design goals first (rather than her business's needs), we were able to design her schedule differently. By limiting her client days to Tuesday, Wednesday, and Thursday, we created extra time for her to leverage her knowledge through creating a DIY course, attending networking events, and doing basic but aligned work around visibility.

After twelve weeks of this approach, Angelica was not only more energized and excited about her life, business, and vision, but she had closed the income gap and enrolled her daughter in her ideal school program.

Where Are You Going, and How Will You Get There?

While core values and your "why" are the flesh and bones of your vision, your goals are the muscle. They get you moving— and, when approached properly, *keep* you moving, even when things get tough.

In this chapter, we will create aligned goals for you to work with in every major area of your life. But first, let's talk a bit about what goals are (and aren't), how they work, and why we have such a love-hate relationship with them.

Goals are *how you keep the promises you made to yourself when creating your vision.*

They are benchmarks—the things you want and need to accomplish along the journey to your dream life. More, they're guidelines for aligned action; they show you when you're on the right track.

Lots of leaders talk about goals. In fact, you've likely had prior experience with goal-setting in other modalities. However, this time is going to be different, because you're coming to the process with a deep sense of purpose and an inner knowing about what you want to create. You understand how you want to show up for yourself and the world at large. In this context, your goals are far more than an arbitrary task list; they're an extension of your core values, "why," and vision!

In this chapter, we are going to work together to set actionable and aligned goals not just for your business and finances, but for every area of your life. These goals will work together synergistically with your vision to create a clear pathway for you to follow as you step into your next stage of expansion.

A few notes before we begin.

The EnVision process begins with a detailed self-assessment. You'll look at seven areas of your life and evaluate how each is stacking up to the life you imagined in your visioning work in Chapter 2.

Then, we'll do a "brain dump" to help you uncover aligned goals for each of the seven areas of your life. I'll share my favorite techniques to help you get the most out of this process.

Finally, we'll use the info you gained in our brain dump to set detailed goals in all areas of your life.

As entrepreneurs, we are always growing, stretching, and learning. Sometimes we focus too heavily on one area—like work—while forgetting about others—like health or spirituality. A lot of times, this comes from a place of fear; we think that if we take our eyes off the prize, our success and profits will evaporate. The EnVision goal-setting process helps alleviate this by creating a set of goals you can easily follow. With some practice, you'll be able to balance all seven areas of your life with greater ease.

Let's begin!

SELF-ASSESSMENT

You can't get where you're going if you don't know where you are.

Working with clients privately and at events, I'm always amazed at the disconnect that exists between our dreams, core values, and "why" as individuals and business owners, and how we are actually operating in our lives. I created this self-assessment practice to help you understand where your energy and attention are going, where your "why" fits into your daily reality, and how to create balance as you Flow and Grow.

So, let's take the pulse of your life. Get out your notebook and pen, and answer this question as truthfully as possible:

On a scale from one to ten, where are you in these key areas of your life?

- Business/Career
- Health/Body
- Emotional well-being
- Spiritual/Personal Growth

- Family

- Friends/Community/Social

- Money/Finances/Stuff

When I introduce this exercise at my EnVision Live events, I ask, "Who feels really balanced in their life?" Almost no hands go up. People get really emotional—and so do I. It makes me sad that we've normalized this level of imbalance for business owners.

At the same time, knowledge is power, and our purpose in this exercise is to create clarity. Don't get down on yourself if you're not in perfect harmony across your whole life. Just be honest and know that when you clearly identify where you want to create change, you can take steps to improve it!

Once you have assessed all seven areas, do some journaling around the following questions:

- "Why did I choose this score for this area of my life?"

- "Where do I want to be in this area?" (Be honest—not every area needs to be of equal priority for you!)

- "How can I best express my core values in this area of my life?"

- "How is this area of my life connected to my 'why'?"

Continue until you have answered the above questions for all seven life areas. You may choose to step away and sit with what you've discovered before coming back to complete the exercise.

THE BRILLIANT BRAIN DUMP

"Brain dumping" is the act of freeing up space in your head by dumping its contents (not literally, of course) onto a sheet of paper. Once all the extra thoughts are out of the way, the brain can focus on what it does best: critical thinking, problem-solving, and turning thoughts into reality.

I've been doing daily brain dumps for years. They help me organize my scurrying thoughts and long to-do lists, which releases the "pressure cooker" feeling in my mind when tasks and deadlines build up over the course of days or weeks.

While this method is great for relieving mental stress and day-to-day overwhelm, it also works wonderfully for goal setting! In this exercise, we'll be doing one brain dump for each of the seven life areas you identified in the self-assessment exercise. To help you get a feel for the process, I've created three sample brain dumps—one each around spirituality/personal growth, material stuff, and money/finances.

A few reminders before we begin:

Your initial responses are nowhere near as important as what the brain dump will trigger later. In fact, you may get your most valuable insights hours after you complete this exercise, while you're driving, in the shower, or while lying in bed.

Write as fast as you can. This isn't about homing in on details. It's about clearing your mind.

There are no "right" answers, only ideas to be explored. Don't allow yourself to indulge in judgment or disbelief, editing, or self-censorship. If you think it, write it!

When you're ready, grab your notebook, pens, and your phone (to use as a timer), and dive in!

Example Brain Dump #1: Spirituality/Personal Growth

In this brain dump, you'll be writing down any goals or aspirations you have in regard to your personal development and spiritual practices.

These goals can be physical, educational, task-oriented, or relationship-oriented. They can be around your business or your personal experience, or both. They can be about what you want to achieve or who you want to become. You're not going for details at this point—just jot down any and all areas that you want to improve in the next one to five years.

When you're ready to begin, set your timer for eight minutes, and don't stop writing until the time is up. If you get stuck, take a quick glance at the prompts below:

- What would you like to learn?
- How do you want to feel about yourself?
- Is there someone you want to study or train with?
- Is there someone you want to meet?
- What are some things you want to learn about?
- What type of books would you like to read this year?
- How many books do you want to read this year?
- What adventures are calling your name?
- What organizations do you want to support, and how?
- How would you like to give and bless others?
- How would you like to lead and inspire others?

Once your time is up, go back and put a timeline (the number 1, 3, 5, or 10) and priority level near each of the goals you brain-dumped. Are these one-year, three-year, five-year, or ten-year goals? Is this a high, medium, or low priority for you?

Example Brain Dump #2: Your "Things" Goals

While technically "things" fall under the same category as money and finances, I like to do a separate brain dump for them—mostly because it's fun!

It may feel materialistic for you to set goals solely around "stuff." If that's true for you, I would encourage you to remember your five-year-old self around your birthday or Christmastime. Did you think about whether Santa or your parents could afford to give you what you asked for? Probably not. You just asked!

That's the way I want you to approach this exercise. Think of the Universe as Santa Claus. Don't allow judgments about your worthiness or current financial state to creep in. This is all about playing in possibility. (PS: if you had a challenging childhood with regard to money or other issues, this is an opportunity to give yourself what you didn't have back then, so go all in.)

Again, I'm going to ask you to write as fast as you can. No judgment. No thoughts about money. No disbelief. If you think it, write it.

Set your timer for eight minutes. When it starts, write down any and all things you want to have, do, or create in the next one to ten years. If you find yourself stuck, come back to this page and take a glance at the prompts:

- What would your ideal home look like? Where is it?
- Do you desire a vacation home? If so, where?

- What kind of car do you want to drive? What color/model/trim package?
- What have you always wanted but never allowed yourself to buy?
- What cities or countries would you love to travel to?
- What concerts or plays do you want to see?
- What clothes, shoes, or jewelry do you want to buy?
- What's your dream vacation?
- What do you want to buy for your spouse?
- What do you want to give to your kids?
- What do you want to give to your community?
- Do you want in-home help—like a nanny, chef, or house cleaner?
- Do you want a personal assistant?
- Do you want a boat? How about a private jet?

Once your time is up, go back and put a timeline (the number 1, 3, 5, or 10) and priority level near each of the goals you brain-dumped. Are these one-year, three-year, five-year, or ten-year goals? Is this a high, medium, or low priority for you?

Example Brain Dump #3: Your Financial Goals

In the financial goals area, I want to encourage you to think in terms of "ages" or chapters of your life. For example, if you desire to have a solid retirement account by age sixty, think about that—but also think about the ages and stages leading up to that.

Again, we're not getting into all the details here. We're also leaving judgment and disbelief by the wayside. Give yourself permission to dream big!

Set your timer for eight minutes. When it starts, write down any and all things you want to have, do, or create in the next one to ten years. If you find yourself stuck, come back to this page and take a glance at the prompts below:

- What are your income goals?
- Debt-crushing goals?
- Business goals?
- Company revenue goals?
- Personal revenue goals?
- Investment goals?
- College savings goals (for yourself or your kids)?
- Goals to find/work with a financial advisor?
- Real estate purchase/investment goals?
- Hiring a coach, advisor, or mentor?
- Tax savings or strategy goals?
- Paying off your mortgage?
- Emergency fund goals?
- Insurance, will, and trust goals?
- Alternative investment goals (cryptocurrency, NFTs, etc.)?

Once your time is up, go back and put a timeline (the number 1, 3, 5, or 10) and priority level near each of the goals you brain-dumped. Are these one-year, three-year, five-year, or ten-year goals? Is this a high, medium, or low priority for you?

SORT AND SET YOUR GOALS

The final step in your goal-setting is to assign your top focus goals for this year.

After your brain dumps, all of your goals should be marked with the number 1, 3, 5, or 10, as well as priorities. From those lists, identify all of your one-year goals that are a high priority for you, and list them on a separate sheet of paper.

You might have six goals on this list, or twenty, or forty. The amount doesn't matter; what matters is that you clarify their order of priority, because from this point forward, 80 percent of your time and focus will go toward the top ten (or top five, if you have fewer than ten) goals on this list.

I do this exercise for myself at least once per year, and I encourage my students to do the same. When I get clear about my vision, my "why," and my goals—when I can see what I want, feel it, taste it, and understand it—I live a richer and more fulfilled life. When I get off-track or overwhelmed, I can see it in my goals. When I'm killing it, I can see that, too!

While some of your goals will be directly related to your business, I'd be willing to bet that most of those you brain-dumped are personal. That's exactly as intended. Our business exists not just to serve others, but to serve us—and when we set boundaries in our business that reflect our personal vision, core values, and goals, we are actually more likely to succeed.

Looking at your personal goals before your business goals allows you to see the specific freedom activators that you hope will come from your business—and, ultimately, see if your business is actually equipped to support your vision. Later, in the Flow Pillar, we'll be looking at the hard numbers to see where and how your personal vision and business structure line up.

Motivation Is Good, but Goals Are Better

Most of my clients don't come to me because they want help claiming their big vision. They come because they're stuck.

Stuck in a foggy vision. Stuck in their revenue flows. Stuck in their ability to attract new clients. Stuck in analysis paralysis. Stuck in debt. Stuck in guilt. Stuck in shame. Stuck in imposter syndrome and the comparison game. Stuck in "not smart enough," "not worthy enough," etc.

Sometimes, this stuckness can feel like a lack of motivation. It's not.

There's a ton of motivational talk in the entrepreneurial world—particularly around goals. *Set them! Expand them! Make them bigger and bolder!* Given how much we hear about motivation, you'd be tempted to think that most people have none!

In my experience, the opposite is true. Most entrepreneurs are highly motivated. However, too much motivation without a clear vision and goals to back it up will create stuckness.

A lot of the time, when people get stuck, it's because they're overworked, overwhelmed, and totally depleted. Maybe you are there, too. Maybe you've read through the information and exercises in this chapter and thought, "This all looks like so much *work*!"

In this state, it's tempting to lay on some more motivation to get yourself over the hump. But what you really need is *clarity*.

Doing the initial work to clarify your vision, "why," and goals will save you massive amounts of time and energy in the long run. How? Imagine if you never wasted a minute focusing on something that wasn't in your one-year plan. Imagine if all of your attention could go toward the goals that matter *right now*, not the stuff that might happen a decade from now. Imagine if setting priorities and making decisions was easier and took less time.

Would that be worth the effort of a few brain dumps and some journaling? I sure hope so!

FACING YOUR "GOAL BLOCKERS"

Right now, you are faced with a choice. Do nothing, and let your life keep spinning out more of the same—or, use what you've learned in these chapters to create a breakthrough. It's up to you.

Chances are, there were two voices shouting inside of you as you read that statement.

One is the voice of fear. Fear (and its cousin, Ego) wants to keep you safe—even if "safe" doesn't look like "happy," or "fulfilled," or even "secure." Fear will always try to talk you out of change.

The other is the voice of your Soul. Your destiny. Your vision. It's the higher part of you—the part that knows what you truly want out of this one and only life, and how to get you there. It says, "Let's go on this great adventure, because all the things we want are right around the corner!"

A good chunk of your success as an entrepreneur will come from learning to navigate between those two voices.

All great spiritual teachers say that self-awareness is the key to growth. That's why it's important to connect to this inner dialogue, rather than just shoving it down into a back corner of your brain. Those two voices in your head actually dictate every action you take in your life. But sometimes, if you're not listening closely, Fear sounds like reason, and Soul sounds like a crazy person. If you don't know which one you're truly listening to, it can be hard to take the leaps necessary to reach your dreams.

So, write down all the nasty things Fear is saying to you. And then, write down what Soul is saying. When a thought comes up over and over, ask:

- Is this really true?
- It is really true that you can't fill all the seats at your show?
- Is it really true that you can't find a way to start that subscription box company you've been dreaming of?
- Is it really true that businesses like yours don't make millions?

If Fear is lying to you, soothe it with evidence. Find examples of other people who are succeeding at exactly what you dream of doing. Then, ask Soul what it has to say.

Fear also loves to get loud around the "how."

It's easy to say, "I want to make $250,000 (or $500,000, or $10,000,000) in revenue this year," or, "I want to work only fifteen hours a week and travel thirty weeks a year." But very few entrepreneurs actually create these kinds of results.

Your goals are meant to be a roadmap to your vision. But a big, ambitious goal with no action plan to back it up isn't a goal. It's a pipe dream.

If you can't clearly identify an action or set of actions that will lead you to your goal, you are far less likely to succeed. This is true for both business and personal goals. So, even if it feels painful, take the time to map out that journey. Even if you only have the first pieces of the "how," it can be enough to soothe that voice of Fear.

Make Your Goals Visible

Humans are visual creatures. When something catches our eye, it commands a lot more of our attention. When we can make our goals visual, they become more "real" in our consciousness, and we feel more accountable to them. There's a reason why Oprah, Tony Robbins, Steve Harvey, and yours truly swear by their vision boards!

Most people's goals never see the light of day. They live in their heads—and often get tucked away in dark corners or passed over when bigger problems arise to be solved. Sure, the goals are there, but they're not *present*, because anything intangible or imaginary is a lower priority for your brain.

So, write your goals down. Post them where you can view them every day. (Bonus points if you read them aloud!) Bring them to life with images and colors. Better yet, make a vision board! (More on how to do this in Chapter 4.) Seeing your goals daily—whether in a list, on a vision board, or in some other format—reminds your mind that these things are top priorities. As we know, our brain loves to solve problems—and, if it is consistently reminded of your goals, it will go to work to meet them.

Get Support to Thrive

After leveraging this powerful work around vision and goals to create new levels of success, I've had multiple clients ask me, with tears in their eyes, "Is it normal that I can clearly see the need to step away from the friend/partner/colleague who can't support me in this?"

This is a painful realization, and it's something visionaries and dreamers deal with a lot. Once we get clearer about our vision, we stop being able to ignore or tolerate the people and situations in our lives that stifle us, hold us back, and just generally make us feel bad. Like Georgia, we realize that it's not okay for people to keep us down, or keep us small—and if we continue to allow them to do so, even if they mean well, we won't fully realize our vision and potential.

The truth is, we all change and grow within the arena of our lives—and sometimes, we need to change who we allow to sit in those front-row seats. Unless they are truly toxic, we don't need to boot them out of our lives altogether—but we can rotate them up to the higher benches to allow more supportive people in. After all, it's your life; you get to decide who gets to cheer you on.

You deserve to be surrounded by people who celebrate you in your success. Finding a community where you can ask questions, feel supported, and be seen for your greatness is vital. I love watching the changemakers in our Envision + Thrive Academy support one another. There is nothing more powerful than being witnessed by people who are not only excited for you but also understand exactly what it took to get to where you are.

If you're feeling like your current "ride or die" crew isn't really along for the ride anymore, you're not alone. Love them for who they are, and love yourself enough to find people who can truly support and inspire you.

CHAPTER 4

Evolving the Vision

BY MONTH NINE of my Freedom Year, I'd come to a point where I was ready to create my "what's next."

Okay, I didn't *exactly* feel ready. It was more a matter of looking at my calendar and saying, "Oh, crap. I'd better figure something out soon!"

But when I leaned into my inner wisdom—which had grown a lot louder and more insistent during my Freedom Year—I realized that I *was* ready, at least to plan.

So, I got out my journals from before my Freedom Year and reread some of my entries. I looked specifically at what I'd written about my visions for achievement, and my longing for balance. Reading through those pages again was instrumental because they reminded me of the discomfort of being out of alignment.

I was creating from a blank slate now, and I was determined not to repeat the same mistakes.

More, I was committed to making an impact in the world. Now that I wasn't locked into one industry or business format, how could I serve others while still using my gifts? When I sat with this, answers arose, and the stepping-stones of my new path began appearing before me.

I had years of financial expertise to offer. My years of entrepreneurial experience taught me a lot about risk management and daily money flows—but that wasn't even the tip of the iceberg. I'd maintained my Investment Advisor licenses for more than two decades. I had a background in tax strategy and preparation. I was constantly taking courses and learning more about money. My own early battles with debt and financial instability showed me the flip side of the coin, and what could happen when entrepreneurs ignored the reality of their financial situation. If I put all of this together, I could create a beautiful shift for entrepreneurs and their families that would teach them strategies they might otherwise never be exposed to or seek out.

I also knew that this format would allow me to build a virtual business. I would have the freedom to work from anywhere, with anyone. Low overhead, high rewards.

And so, Sick of The Hustle Financial Coaching was born.

Tapping into my existing network meant lots of initial connections, which was great. I wasn't looking for any one demographic to begin with—as part of my ongoing commitment to listen to divine inner guidance, I was 100 percent open to whatever and whoever showed up. Taking a page from *A Course in Miracles*, I began each day with a short prayer: "Where would you have me go? What would you have me do? What would you have me say, and to whom?"

I coached couples who had heard about my work or who had come through one of my Financial Peace University classes. I coached recent college grads who wanted to free themselves from the chains of student loan debt. I coached brand new entrepreneurs and established business owners. But by far the biggest and most obvious group of people seeking my services were divorced women.

I took this as a sign and decided to become a resource for these women. Most were three to five years post-divorce and struggling with financial instability. Many hadn't handled the money in their marriages. They were underwater, unable to breathe, and scared because everything they'd built with their former spouse was now split in half—or worse, gone entirely. Some were using credit cards to stay afloat and maintain the "norms" their kids were accustomed to in an effort to ease the pain of the split, and then panicking as they watched their credit card balances continue to rise.

I wanted to help these women so much. I knew my twenty-three years of financial expertise could mean the difference between surviving and thriving for so many of them. I decided to educate myself around collaborative divorce processes and earned my designation as a Certified Divorce Financial Analyst. My free Facebook group soon attracted more than 2,000 women. In May 2016, I self-published a white paper titled "5 Things You Must Know Before Signing a Divorce Settlement". In 2018, I published my first book, *Prosperity After Divorce*, which went on to become a national bestseller on Amazon and has remained on Amazon's Top 100 lists for more than four years. That book outlined my process for LifeStyle Redesign Planning and how that process could help women master life's planned—and unplanned—transitions. Soon, I was speaking regularly to audiences of women around the country.

I created all the foundational infrastructure necessary to support the women I wanted to help: my free group, a free webinar that would lead them to my work and help them reset their LifeStyle pillars, a five-week online virtual workshop, and of course, one-to-one programs to support those who wanted me to walk them through the process personally. I was also taking on case work as part of the Collaborative Divorce team, and working with clients as a Certified Divorce Financial Analyst to dig into their numbers and find the most equitable pathway for them to leave their marriages without ending up in poverty.

I launched *so many things* in three years, following my inner nudges and what I thought was clear divine guidance. But along the way, I forgot to build in my personal vision. Focused on serving and delivering, I lost track of my own life.

The result? I was absolutely exhausted.

Once again, I was working six days a week and putting in twelve-hour days. I hardly noticed this at first because I was so excited to be building something so impactful—but the grind soon caught up with me.

The last straw was when I agreed to host my virtual Mastering Your Next Chapter workshop on a Sunday evening, because that's what women were asking for. Sundays were supposed to be my family days. Jody (my new husband) and I hosted boisterous family dinners in the fall and winter, and coordinated beach days in the summer. Now, I was rushing my family out the door to hop into my Zoom room and lead eight women through their next Pillar.

Everyone tells you to "niche down" to succeed. But as I did more and more work in the arena of divorce, my inner energy coffers, as well as my personal financial coffers, were running dry. Many of the women I was helping were not fully ready to do this work. They hadn't yet come to terms with the challenges of their new realities. They were not ready to trust themselves to follow the advice and strategies I knew would help them. They were reaching out, but not committing to the path. As a result, I was chasing payments, barely getting by, and burning through my savings to make it all work—and, the whole time, judging myself for being a financial coach who wasn't making money.

I thought maybe this was a test of my faith. Maybe God wanted to see if my heart was really in this work. I had come to this chapter in my life knowing it would be about service and passion—would I really give up so easily?

Yet, would God *really* ask me to give up precious moments with my kids? Was it *really* in divine alignment to forego my self-care, my joy, and my all-important freedom so that I could support women to create a future they weren't ready to claim for themselves?

And, most of all, was I really practicing what I preached?

How many of us fall into this trap? How many of us think that service *must* equal hustle, grind, and suffering? How many of us think that we have to pay a price for our vision—that we can't truly have it all?

After many moments of reflection, self-doubt, and deep listening, I realized that what I had wasn't a failure, but rather a crop that was not growing. I had tilled, planted, and watered the seed of this purpose with my time, money, and energy for three years, but I had more weeds in my field than flowers, and eventually, I was going to run out of water.

The problem wasn't my clients—they were showing up authentically and to the best of their abilities, and I loved each and every one of them. The problem was that, as someone who had been there, done that, and thrived in the end, I saw possibilities that weren't yet clear to them. As a result, I was trying to create something they weren't ready for and force it to work for all of us. I saw so much potential in that space, but that didn't mean the potential was ready to bloom.

It wasn't failure; it was simply wrong timing.

And if I wanted to truly serve—in alignment with my own biggest gifts and highest potential—I needed to create a business that supported my biggest vision for my life.

Sometimes in our exploration, we need to create in order to un-create. We need to learn more about who we are, what we like and don't like, and what will actually work for us. Sometimes, we need to recreate old patterns in order to break them once and for all. Sometimes, we need to build the thing only to watch it topple.

How to Have It All

During my time as a financial coach for divorced women, I put many of my gifts on the shelf. I sidelined my experience as a business owner and entrepreneur. I made my gifts of planning and analysis secondary, rather than equal to, my gifts of vision and strategy. I didn't talk about vision boards, or the way I planned and created my life; they seemed secondary now to the concerns I was addressing. I kept glancing at those parts of me in my rearview mirror, thinking they belonged to my previous chapter of life.

When I hit the proverbial wall, I had to make a new decision. I had to decide that it was okay to take another road without changing the destination. A road that would align all of who I was as a person—including my vision for my life and for the lifestyle I wanted to be living—with the ways I wanted to serve in the world.

It was time to marry my vision with my business.

More, it was time to harness all my various gifts within my business so I could be *all of who I am*, all the time.

Often, when we make a big change—like starting a business after a corporate career, or starting a new business after an old one goes sideways—it's tempting to think we have to put some of our gifts and talents on a shelf and focus on a new expression. Don't get me wrong, it's important to grow and change. But denying or ignoring your greatest strengths because you don't want to use them in the same way anymore isn't the solution. I've seen fabulous strategists sideline their gifts in their coaching businesses because they didn't want to be seen as "too analytical." I've seen amazing visionaries create "backstage" roles for themselves because that's what they believed their industry demanded. After a while, denying your true strengths catches up with you—whether it's through burnout or dissatisfaction.

Chances are, the vision you've created for your life, and the goals that you've set as part of that vision, will not only encourage you to bring all your gifts and talents to the forefront; they will *require* it. Your most powerful contributions will always be made at the intersection of your purpose, your values, and your greatest gifts.

After taking some time to grieve the path my work in the divorce space had taken, I decided to try something new—something that would speak to entrepreneurs like me who were having challenges around creating a business and life that worked together.

Of course, the first thing I did was to update my vision to match what was brewing inside me. I "retreated" myself and created space to see what I could create if I opened myself to this new possibility. I journaled. How did I want to show up in this new expression? Where and how did I want to say yes—and where did I need to say no?

A picture began to emerge. Immediately, I got to work creating a vision board as a visual representation of my new path.

While sorting through piles of materials in search of one particular image, I suddenly thought, "Why not do a one-day vision board workshop for entrepreneurs?" In a workshop format, I could share the true process of how I did my yearly business planning, and everything I'd done over the last three decades to hone my own process for strategic planning, goal-setting, and vision creation. I could show them how to set revenue goals based on their desired lifestyle, not just their business model. These things were the foundation of my own business success, and I wanted to share them *all*.

I didn't want this to be just another "vision board party," though. I wanted it to be something more. I wanted the entrepreneurs who attended this workshop to walk away with a completely new vision around what was possible in their lives and businesses—and with clarity around how to execute on that vision.

I decided that I would call this event "EnVision," since it had come to me while I was, once again, in the mix of envisioning my ideal life and business.

My first step was to book a room that could hold forty people—my ideal number of attendees. I would have about twelve weeks to bring this to life—and I was committed.

I didn't create sales pages, fancy funnels, or an email series. I simply let my network know that I was "considering" hosting an event, and started a waitlist. For the next three weeks, I talked about EnVision with everyone I came into contact with—again, not as a pitch, but from an "I'm thinking about this" angle. I figured that if the idea didn't land, I could revise the workshop topic. I also offered to speak at local chapters of networking organizations, where more people signed up for the waitlist.

Then, once the registration page was live, I sent an email to those on the waitlist, and to everyone in my professional network. Within three days of sending that invitation, the workshop was sold out, with eleven people on a waitlist.

So, I chose another date and booked a second event. Again, it sold out. I was beyond excited.

At the first workshop during the afternoon break, eight attendees approached me to ask, "How can I have your help in my business?" These individuals had big goals and believed

I could help them get there. I was totally taken aback. I hadn't positioned myself as a "business coach." And yet, I'd guided entrepreneurs as an insurance agent for years. Conversations about business cycles, revenue goals, and marketing were second nature for me. And, thanks to my time supporting divorced women, so were conversations about vision, lifestyle design, and overcoming limiting beliefs.

In a split second, I realized that everything in my life thus far had been leading me to *this*. This moment. This opportunity. I was more than equipped, more than qualified.

I was honored to share my process—but more, I was doing so in a way that felt exciting to me. I was in awe of the energy in those rooms. I was lit up all day long supporting these groups of like-minded entrepreneurs through the process I'd created for myself. If ever I had experienced "alignment," this was it.

I could. I should. I *must*.

At the close of these workshops, I invited my attendees to allow me to support them more deeply through one-on-one VIP days. Those sold out, too.

And so, EnVision was born.

I will always be grateful to those first two groups of entrepreneurs who said yes to my invitation to those workshops. They got a lot more than poster boards and glue sticks during our time together—and so did I.

Today, more than 500 people have come through my annual EnVision events—even with a global pandemic and all the challenges it presented. I've served up support to thousands of entrepreneurs through virtual and in-person offerings, helping them get clear about their vision, their cash flow planning, and their strategic footprint for visibility in their businesses.

But the best part is that the business is unfolding in perfect alignment with my vision for my life.

Make Your Vision Real with a Vision Board

It's time to take everything you've learned in the last few chapters and put it all together on a single, powerful vision board.

If you haven't already guessed, I am a *huge* fan of vision boards. I made my first one at the age of nineteen and have created thirteen more since—one every three years—as well as numerous smaller, goal-specific vision boards. Heck, I even have a board specifically for this book! (If you're wondering, it's covered in words like "*Bestseller! Awards! Events! Retreats!*" along with photos of the global media superstars I will be interviewed by.)

So many amazing manifestations have come about as a result of my vision boards, even if they didn't appear as expected. Like the time I pasted a luxury convertible on my board and Jody and my son surprised me with a new car in the same style after my son's car died. Their plan was for my son to take over my current car and me to get my dream car. Just before they unveiled the surprise, Jody went into my office and put a Post-It over the car on my vision board with a heart and the word "DONE." What was also funny was that the word "SURPRISE!" was on that board in the *same* corner just an inch from the photo of the luxury convertible pasted there, as I wanted to invite more fun and spontaneity into my life. Well, the car was certainly a surprise!

Now that you have created your aligned Vision Statement, identified your values, found your "why," and set aligned goals, you're ready to craft a powerful visual depiction of all the amazingness you are inviting into your life and business.

My preferred method is super old-school, with poster board, glue sticks, old magazines (check with your local library as they often give their outdated ones away), and other tangible elements. Or you can create a digital vision board using a tool like Pinterest or Canva, and have it printed at your local office supply store.

Start with the feelings you want to feel. Let those take up the most space. Then, incorporate visual elements from the goals you set in Steps 2 and 3. (As I mentioned earlier, there's nothing wrong with having material goals, as long as they don't overshadow the feelings!) Play with this. Move things around before you glue them into place. Layer the truths, concepts, and magic you want to experience in your life. You'll feel it when it's right.

I do three-year vision boards so I can incorporate longer-term goals. Some people prefer one-year boards. Do what works for you. Just don't cram in so much that you start to feel doubt around receiving it all. Remember, this is a visual representation of what you have decided to create in your life, not a collage of "have-tos." The energy of it is important.

Hang your vision board on a wall where you will see it every day. Mine is in my office; when I glance up from my laptop, it's the first thing I see. Know that everything on that board is possible for you, starting *now*.

Your Vision Paves Your Path to Profits

We are so often told, "Go where you're led." And it's true—but with a caveat.

I say, "Define your vision first. Then, set goals. Then, go where *aligned* opportunities lead you."

Sometimes, we forget that we have the power to order up whatever we want from the Universe. Manifestation and creation aren't about instant results, but rather about curating aligned next steps and opportunities. When we use our vision to define our boundaries and inform our decisions, we can steer the boat of our business in the direction of our dream life.

But if you take your hands off the wheel, you could end up anywhere.

I learned that the hard way. I went where I was led—but I forgot to set the parameters first. I set material goals, but not goals around my priorities and how I wanted to experience my life. I said yes to things that were totally out of alignment with my values (Sunday night workshops? What was I thinking?). I knew that these choices were compromising my vision for my business and life, but I believed the sacrifice was worth it—that they would eventually lead me to what I truly wanted.

As I soon learned, that's not how it works.

When we say yes to something, we are telling the Universe, "More of this, please!" And when we say no, we say, "That isn't acceptable to me. Let's try something else."

If you are like me (and like most entrepreneurs), you've chased opportunities and made decisions in pursuit of business success without weighing them against your vision for your life. Maybe, like Leslie from Chapter 2, you've been chasing success without any vision in place at all. Maybe, like me in my Prosperity After Divorce days, you've been following a path of service without considering how to fill your own cup, too. Or maybe you're already super successful but feel like your whole life is constantly put on hold because the business comes first.

The good news is, it's never too late to create alignment.

Alignment requires two things: vision and goals. Thankfully, you have both of those powerhouse tools in your corner now. However, as you may have already discovered for yourself, sometimes creating alignment *also* requires radical change and restructuring. Of course, this is not always the case—but if you've been struggling to make your values and goals align within your current business model, you may be standing at this crossroads. This need for alignment will become even more clear as we move forward into the Flow Pillar.

Your version of alignment will be unique to you—and, make no mistake, it will require you to be fully present, engaged, committed, and open to evolution. Maybe, like me, you'll need to reexamine how, when, where, and with whom you are working within your current business model. Or, maybe it's time to create an entirely new business model that uses all of your most potent skills and talents.

I can't offer advice for your unique situation in the context of this book, as there are literally millions of scenarios across thousands of business models we could cover. I can, however, offer a simple process to guide you as you lean into and assess your current reality. It involves three lines of inquiry:

1. Where does my business align with my values, "why," and goals, and where do they diverge?

2. Is my business *actually capable* of supporting the life I truly desire?

3. If yes, what's working, and what needs to change? If no, what business model *will* create that foundation for me?

These are powerful questions. If you take your time with them, answer as honestly as you can, and journal about what comes up for you, you will soon begin to see a new path. If you still feel stuck, I suggest engaging a qualified business advisor to help you explore your next steps.

It All Comes Back Around

In those dark and desperate days when Prosperity After Divorce began to collapse, I had no idea how everything would play out. I still wanted to serve the women I knew could benefit from my experience. But building a business around them was clearly no longer the right path.

I had done all I could for the moment. The book was in the world, empowering people every day. I was still receiving handwritten notes, emails, and reviews from people whose lives had been changed by the work. The Master Your Next Chapter masterclass became a self-paced, DIY course that could support people at an accessible price point that allowed them to take what they needed, when they needed it; a percentage of the profits from that course would be donated to support divorced and divorcing women with financial literacy and empowerment.

I could no longer pour all my life force into that business, but I didn't have to abandon my community there.

Every day, even after EnVision began to take shape, I would lean into my higher power and offer up a prayer:

I am here to serve. I am here to be a light. When I'm ready to do that with Prosperity After Divorce, please present the opportunities and I will answer the call.

And then, nearly four years after the book was published, and more than three years after the creation of EnVision and my shift into financial consulting and Business Profitability Strategy, I was interviewed by *Parents* magazine about Prosperity After Divorce. The interview did well and was picked up by *People*. Suddenly, my inbox was flooded with requests to learn more about how I could support divorced women. My prayers were answered—and my vision was coming true in complete alignment with the goals I set for my business and my life. By sticking to my goals and vision for my life, even when it felt hard and painful to do so, I opened the door for aligned success.

Prosperity After Divorce is no longer my primary offer. However, the work I've done to align my vision for my life with my business—including the creation of EnVision—has allowed me to offer divorce support in a way that is truly a gift and a service. Now that I have the financial flow and flexibility of a thriving business, I am no longer burned out and frustrated. Prosperity After Divorce is becoming the philanthropic arm of my work—a gift from my heart, rather than a financially-generative offer.

As your business grows and evolves, you will need to continually revisit and evolve your personal vision to keep aligning your business with your vision for your life.

As you do this, it may be necessary to let go of values, goals, or aspects of your business that no longer serve you. While this can be painful, remember that nothing is wasted. Everything comes back around—whether as lessons that inform your next steps, or as new opportunities that allow you to grow into the fullness of your purpose—and your past efforts *will* return to you as blessings, as long as you are open to receive them.

PILLAR II
Flow

CHAPTER 5
Getting Real

WHEN I CO-OWNED my insurance company, I had lots of money but no time freedom. When I started my journey as an advisor for divorced women, I had very little cash flow ... and I still had no time freedom.

When I designed EnVision and built my current business, I knew I wanted to have it all. I wanted money freedom. I wanted time freedom. I wanted to know that I could put my life first and still make it all work.

In order to do that, I *needed* the numbers. I needed to know *exactly* how much money I was receiving, and where it was coming from. I also needed to know what my real expenses were (both personal and business). I needed to figure out what my dream life *actually cost*. Only then could I determine how to design my business, price my services, and create the flow that would support my vision.

That's what the Flow Pillar is all about. *Money* flow. *Energy* flow. *Time* flow.

The flow of your dream life.

I love working in the Flow space. While Vision sets the stage, Flow is where dreams ignite. It's where legacies are born. And yet, Flow is the hardest part of the EnVision process for many, because in order to Flow, we have to *know*—

And knowing begins with the big, bad B-word: *Budget*.

If you just cringed, you're not alone. Most people look forward to budget planning about as much as they look forward to dental work. In fact, many of my clients would rather have their teeth pulled without Novocaine than actually look at their numbers! There are many reasons for this, from childhood money trauma to shame over past financial decisions, but the results of financial avoidance are always the same: missed opportunities, misaligned spending, and a lack of financial stability.

Most entrepreneurs I meet are making decisions based on their daily bank balance, not a long-term strategy. Many of them aren't even taking a salary! They have no real idea what's moving in and out of their bank accounts, and so every day feels like walking a tightrope. You can't dream bigger if you don't know where your next mortgage payment is coming from, or if you'll be able to make payroll this week. You can't feel abundant and financially free if you can't meet your basic needs, or if you're barely breaking even each month.

Simply put, if you won't look at the money flows, don't expect the money to grow!

Here's the thing: numbers are neutral. They only have as

much emotional meaning as you assign to them. More, numbers help you make choices based on what's actually happening in your life and business (as opposed to what you wish or hope is happening). You need to know exactly where you are and exactly where you want to be so you can make a plan to get from here to there. As my story and the other stories I've shared in this book prove, what you aren't willing to see *will* come back to haunt you.

If you're not in an ideal place right now, that's okay! I've got your back. There is always a way out if you're willing to make the climb. So set aside any uncomfortable feelings and fears you may be struggling with, take a deep breath, and repeat after me:

"In order to Flow, I need to *know*."

LifeStyle Design Planning

When I stepped off the stage at my opening EnVision event, Rhonda Miller was the first person to meet me at the back of the room.

"I'm going to work with you. Take this application before I change my mind!" she told me.

I loved her zeal. More, I loved her desire to do what it took to uplevel her business.

When we dug into the vision exercises she'd completed at the EnVision event, it was clear to me that she had gained clarity around building a life she loved, rather than just a business that would pay the bills. She was on a great trajectory: she and her husband, Jeff (who had a steady job in a staffing firm), had been following Dave Ramsey's program for a few years on their own, and they had a solid plan in place to take ownership of their financial future. Now, Rhonda wanted to create a pathway for her business to accelerate their timelines.

Even though Rhonda had been through the Vision Pillar exercises at the EnVision event, we agreed that the best place for us to start was a goal-setting session for her and her husband as a team. She could use that session to share her vision and goals with him, and he could do the same by completing some of the exercises on his own before the call.

Rhonda and Jeff didn't have quite the same level of resistance as others when we started working together because they had already been following an envelope system and were used to monthly spending plans. However, working with the EnVision Flow Pillar did what their current budgeting system could not: it revealed the relationship between Rhonda's business and their personal financial goals.

As it turned out, Rhonda had much bigger financial dreams than Jeff did. She had a deep desire for the luxuries in life; they were, she shared, "proof" of all her hard work. In particular, she wanted to travel four to six times a year—two family trips with Jeff and the kids, two romantic trips for her and Jeff, and two trips alone or with friends.

Jeff, on the other hand, was a minimalist. He didn't understand Rhonda's desire for a fancy car, expensive shoes, a bigger home, or international travel. Instead of spending on "nice-to-haves," he wanted to put all their extra cash toward retirement.

Up until we started working together, Rhonda had gone along with this, because she didn't feel her business could bring in enough cash to match her vision. However, she was feeling stifled by their current budget, and resentful that she couldn't enjoy the money she was earning.

As we went over their individual and shared visions, we assigned price tags to every possible spending item in their personal financial realm. We mapped out not only "survival" expenses like food, mortgage payments, taxes, retirement savings, car payments, gas, and other necessities, but also "desire items" like the upgraded cars, new home, luxury goods, debt repayment, and increased IRA funding. Then, we assigned costs to every one of their top ten dreams.

The Millers already had a good idea what the first set of costs looked like. But when we factored in the "desires" and "goals" costs, we got a much fuller picture of what was possible—and what was needed to bridge the gap between where they were and where they wanted to be. Finally, they could see beyond just paying down credit card debt and their hefty student loans. They began to see their financial goals in layers, and found mutual goals that excited them and felt achievable. Both of them could have what they wanted, without the pressure being on just one person.

This is the gift of LifeStyle Design Planning. It isn't about just redistributing what you have. It's about creating flow, plugging holes, and setting goals so you can have it *all*.

Many spiritual teachers remind us, "Where attention goes, energy flows." If you put your attention on meeting your financial goals, and anchor that energy with hard numbers and timelines, you are more likely to get where you want to go.

In this chapter, we'll dive into your personal and business numbers and see where you currently stand. As a parallel, I'll be sharing Rhonda and Jeff's spreadsheets so you can see the planning systems in action. Then, in Chapter 6, we'll map out the money flows for your dream life and make a plan to bridge the gap.

But, before we delve into the details, let's tackle the elephant in the room: your money story.

YOUR MONEY STORY

Your money story is the total package of your beliefs about what money is, how it flows, who has it, and whether it likes you. It's the story of how you *relate* to money—and it has a huge impact on your experience of entrepreneurship, particularly in times of instability or upheaval.

Your money story will determine whether you love budgeting and forecasting or loathe it, whether you overspend or over-save, whether you stay on top of every penny or prefer to save your Profit & Loss (P&L) reports for tax day. It also determines whether you believe you can have a different experience of money than you're having now.

Chances are, you went deep into your money story the moment I mentioned "budgeting." You might be telling yourself why you can't or shouldn't make a budget, why you couldn't or shouldn't assess cash flows in your business, or why you should or shouldn't be where you are financially. Maybe you're listing to yourself all the things you don't understand about money. Maybe you're telling yourself, "I'm smart. I don't need basic crap like spreadsheets."

Maybe you're just swearing at me in your head. (Don't worry, I won't hold it against you!)

Everyone has "money stuff." Fear and money, for most people, are practically joined at the hip. But if you want to get on the Path to Profits, changing your unhelpful money stories isn't optional. If you keep doing what you've always done, you'll get what you've always gotten.

If you're running into major resistance, try the reframes below before moving on to the exercises. I created them based on the most common money stories my clients share with me. Some may resonate, while others may not; only use the ones that feel helpful to you. Approaching these shifts as questions (first option) allows your brain to interact with them differently. Ask your brain to allow that these are possibilities—that they might be true, just as your current money story might be true. Then, once your brain has accepted the possibility of a new truth, use the second option as an affirmation to cement a new belief.

Money Reframe Questions:

- "Is it possible to have a healthy, positive relationship with money?" / "I have a healthy and positive relationship with money!"

- "What would make it possible for me to trust myself with money?" / "I trust myself to handle money wisely."

- "Is it possible that creating [X dollars] a month in revenue could be easy?" / "It is easy and fun to create [X dollars] a month in revenue!"

- Is it true that it's difficult to make money consistently?" / "Money flows to me consistently and with ease."

Create your own questions and affirmations to support the shift you want to make in your own money story. Remember, opening your mind to *possibility* first is key.

GETTING THE NUMBERS DOWN

Now, it's time to get down to business—the business of your life, that is.

This exercise is all about your personal money flows as they stand right now. So, find all your bank, credit card, and other billing statements (or download your electronic ones), and get ready to dig in. (Go to www.MichelleJacobik.com/PathtoProfitsResources to download your interactive LifeStyle Design spreadsheets!)

Step 1: Your Income

We are listing income that does not come from your business in this first exercise so we can see exactly how much your business needs to generate to support your lifestyle. Even if you take a W-2 salary from your business, don't include it here.

Using separate lines on a notebook or spreadsheet for each category, list out your income sources.

- Net income from employment (meaning, from a job that isn't your business, or from a partner or spouse)
- Child support income
- Alimony income
- Pensions, retirement distributions, social security, or settlement income
- Investment income/dividends

- Rental income (this should be the net amount that you bring into your personal accounts after expenses are paid, after you've put aside enough cash for normal upkeep, taxes, insurance, etc.; and after you have saved enough to cover three months of property-related expenses and any future planned improvements or repairs. If you don't have these things already in place, don't count your rental income in these totals)

- Other income (gig work, freelancing, Uber/Lyft driving.)

Step 2: Your Expenses

In this section, we'll chart every penny that leaves your personal accounts. Be honest—and if you're not sure, estimate on the high end.

- *Housing Expenses.* Mortgage payment/rent, insurance, taxes, utilities/heating (electric, gas, oil, wood, pellets, water), trash/recycling, internet, cable TV, phone, cell phones and data plans, home upkeep, repairs and maintenance, alarm services, and special projects.

- *Debt repayments.* Note minimum payment amounts for all personal debts, including: personal credit cards, store cards, auto loans, personal loans, student loans, and loans from family and friends. (Note: If you want to pay more than your minimum payments, you can identify that amount once you have the full picture of your lifestyle budget. For now, just write down what you need to pay.)

- *Seasonal purchases.* Think about everything you do in your yard and how you decorate for each season/holiday. Include items like: lawn care services, indoor and outdoor plants, starter plants and seeds, gardening supplies, mulch, snow removal services, outdoor decorations, and holiday decorations. If you have a pool or spa, don't forget chemicals, water testing, filling, maintenance, repairs, and opening/closing costs.

- *Transportation expenses.* Car loans; gas; insurance; taxes; registration fees; license renewal fees; repairs and maintenance; car washes; AAA subscriptions; tolls; subway, bus, and train fares; personal Uber, Lyft, and taxi fees.

- *Food and household items.* Groceries (estimate weekly on the high end), cleaning products and supplies, laundry supplies, paper goods.

- *Eating out.* Restaurant meals, coffee, fast food, drive-thru stops, and takeout (including delivery like Uber Eats/ Grub Hub).

- *Clothing and accessories.* This segment is all about planning and what your budget can handle. Think seasonally and also about your needs versus your wants. Clean out your closet and consign things you no longer wear. (You can get some money back!) Set aside a fixed amount for "must-haves" and another amount for impulse spending.

- *Medical, dental, vision, and health.* Health insurance (if it isn't already deducted from your paycheck or paid as a business expense through the business); HSA funding; gym memberships; exercise classes and subscriptions; chiropractic care; physical therapy and other bodywork;

acupuncture, energy work, and other holistic care; co-pays for doctors, specialists, therapists, etc.; vitamins and supplements; vision costs (glasses, contact lenses and supplies, etc.); dental expenses (cleanings, fillings, ortho-dontist visits).

- *Personal care expenses.* I like to see clients break these out instead of lumping them into their grocery costs, even if they're buying products at the supermarket. It's helpful to see what you're spending on personal care versus food. In this category, include: haircuts, color, and styling; shampoo, conditioner, body wash, and other shower products; facial care products; lotion, oils, and other body care products; shaving products; toothpaste, toothbrushes, mouthwash and floss; other personal care products.

- *Spending money.* What nonessential expenses will you include in your monthly budget? Think manicures and pedicures, salon visits, non-medical massage and body-work, facials and spa treatments, your daily mocha latte, yoga or Pilates classes, golf memberships, club dues, dining out, beach or park access and parking fees.

- *Travel & Recreation.* Vacations (flights, hotels, food costs, and souvenirs), travel insurance, RV/camper costs, boat repairs, marina fees, timeshare fees, retreats, and work-shops that are non-business related.

- *Kids' expenses.* Clothing, shoes, socks, underwear, and accessories (budget monthly if they are still growing, quar-terly if they are not); diapers and diapering supplies; toys and games; sports, dance, martial arts, and other activity costs; uniforms, gear, and travel fees; tuition costs; school lunches; daycare and babysitters; after-school programs;

field trips; summer camps and vacation camps; fundraisers; tutors; private lessons; religious education costs; Halloween costumes, allowance and "commissions" for doing chores. (Note: track these expenses separately if you are sharing costs per a divorce agreement.)

- *Pets.* Pet food; pet toys; collars, leashes, sweaters, and other gear; vet visits (routine and emergency); pet licenses and insurance; grooming; flea, tick, and heartworm treatments; specialty treats; doggy daycare, dog walkers/sitters, poop cleanup service, kenneling fees (if you haven't factored them into your vacation budget).

- *Gifts.* Make a list of all the people you buy for on a yearly basis, including: children, grandchildren, other family (siblings, aunts, uncles, nieces, nephews, etc.), friends, coworkers, kids' teachers and coaches, babysitters, other care providers (nurses, home care aides, etc.), and service providers (your hairdresser, esthetician, mail carrier, etc.). Then, after making your list of recipients, pull out your calendar and make a list of the occasions you buy for, like: birthdays, Christmas, Hanukkah, Easter, Passover, Valentine's Day, Halloween, Mother's Day, Father's Day, weddings and wedding showers, baby showers, housewarming parties, and kids' birthday parties. Most of my clients tell me that their gifting costs about $500 a year—when, in reality, it's more like $3,000!

- *Charity/donations.* Think seasonally as well here. Leave out payroll-deducted charitable giving as that is already subtracted from your monthly income, but include: tithing, monthly donations, adopting a family for the holidays, GoFundMe donations, etc.

- *Savings.* Include only items that are not deducted from your weekly paychecks, such as 401(k)/IRA contributions, whole life insurance, etc. Any other savings activity will be based on where you are in the Path to Profits that you will learn in Step 3 of this exercise, and how much you have to work within your budget each month.

- *Future planned spending.* Do you have any large expenses coming up that you aren't currently paying for—like college tuition, major home renovations/repairs, or helping a relative with a loan? Include those, too!

- *Miscellaneous.* Include any expenses that don't fit into the above categories, like child support, spousal maintenance payments, property settlement payments, dry cleaning, ATM fees, etc. If you have hobbies or recreational equipment not included above, start a new category!

When we broke down the Millers' income and expenses, the numbers looked like this:

Step 3: Your LifeStyle Revealed!

Get out your calculator, my friend. It's time to do the math.

First, add up all the "income" categories to get your average monthly income flow. Then, add up all your "expense" categories to get the average monthly outflow. This will give you an idea of what you should have left after all expenses have been paid. (You can also multiply both numbers by twelve to get your yearly averages.)

Since you didn't include any of the current income from your business, this number might be negative. That's okay! What this exercise is meant to show you is *the minimum*

Expenses by category	$/month	$/year
Current monthly bills inc. credit card minimums, utilities, mortgage	$4,167	$50,000
Digital entertainment	$50	$600
Heating oil (saving for fall/winter	$110	$1,320
Groceries & Household	$850	$10,200
Work lunches	$200	$2,400
Trash (quarterly)	$50	$200
Home upkeep	$125	$1,500
Auto repairs/upkeep	$20	$240
Credit card mins & other debts	$615	$7,380
Medical insurance and copays	$570	$6,840
Car taxes/registration/license	$20	$240
Vacation fund	$250	$3,000
Personal care/haircuts	$40	$480
Gas, Uber, EZ-Pass,	$60	$720
Entertainment	$400	$4,800
Yoga & fitness classes	$40	$480
Christmas gifts	$150	$1,800
Other gifts (birthdays, weddings, etc.)	$65	$785
Kids' spending/entertainment	$75	$900
Kids' field trips, school supplies, etc.	$60	$720
Minimum Lifestyle Cost (MLC) total	**$7,917**	**$95,000**

take-home required from you and your business. We'll call this number your Minimum Lifestyle Cost or MLC.

Are you able to maintain your lifestyle without a steady

Know Your Numbers

Minimum Lifestyle Cost (MLC)
= Total monthly recurring and
non-recurring expenses needed
to maintain your lifestyle

paycheck from your business? If so, for how long? If not, what size paycheck *is* required from you and your business to maintain your current lifestyle without using credit cards, draining savings accounts, or taking on other debt?

Again, we're looking only at current numbers here. In Chapter 6, I'll show you how to create not one but five revenue goals to activate your vision, meet your personal goals, pay down debts, and more. Remember, the clearer you get about what you want to create, the easier it is to create it. The vision activates the money!

Business Design Planning

Now, it's time to look at the other side of the coin: your business!

We will take the same basic approach here as we did for your personal numbers. We'll put the magnifying lens on your business expenses so we have a clear idea of what it costs each month and year to keep the business running. This time, however, we will leave out the "income" portion and just focus on the "expense" portion.

RECURRING MONTHLY EXPENSES

Some expenses occur predictably every month, such as:

- *Employee expenses.* Payroll, health insurance, 401k or IRA payments, payroll taxes, etc. (Remember that some months may have five weeks, so divide your annual number by twelve to get an average month.)

- *Physical location.* Mortgage or rent payments, membership to a co-working space (like WeWork), property taxes, if applicable, cleaning services, extermination etc.

- *Insurance.* Health insurance and ancillary benefits, property coverage, business liability, including errors and omissions, if applicable, and ancillary business protection, such as data breach coverage, product recall, company car insurance, etc.

- *Transportation and shipping.* Is there a budgeted line item for getting your goods to your warehouse, etc?

- *Auto expenses.* Gas, auto loans or leases, maintenance and repair costs, tax and registration, etc.

- *Travel.* Airline tickets, hotel costs, meals and entertainment related to business travel, rental cars, train and bus tickets, visa fees, etc.

- *Equipment.* Leases, loans, maintenance and parts, transportation, etc.

- *Banking and credit cards.* Credit card processing fees, credit card interest payments, bank fees, lines of credit, etc.

- *Utilities.* Phone systems, alarm systems, cell phone and data bills, internet, electric, gas, trash, recycle, shredding services.

- *Subscriptions.* Online software, association dues and subscriptions, networking memberships, etc.

- *Production of goods, packaging, and shipping.*

- *Accounting and legal.* Tax preparation fees, monthly bookkeeping, lawyers' retainers, etc.

- *Future planned expenses.* Add any planned spending for upcoming expansions, purchases, equipment, coaching investments, travel, etc. that doesn't already show up in your budget.

- *Tax expenses.* Depending on your corporate structure, you will likely need to pay taxes on your business income. Work with your tax professional to get accurate estimates or percentages for your business type. Knowing your marginal tax rate and having a CPA in an advisory role (rather than just a tax preparation role) will help you get this right. When in doubt, consider allocating 25–30 percent of gross revenue to tax expenses; if you end up overcalculating, you can move those dollars toward savings, investments, or your retirement accounts at the end of the year!*

I know every business is different, so assume I've left something out and lift your own hood to be sure we didn't miss anything related to your business/industry.

---

* Go to www.MichelleJacobik.com/PathtoProfitsResources to download interactive spreadsheets!

Operating costs	$/month	$/year
Current monthly bills including credit card minimums, utilities, rent	$3,107	$37,284
Gas	$250	$3,000
Supplies and shipping	$265	$3,180
Listing expenses	$550	$6,600
Conferences/travel	$400	$4,800
Dues, subscriptions, insurance	$266	$3,192
Training and education	$180	$2,160
Annual retreat/summit	$185	$2,220
Networking connectioions	$180	$2,160
Networking events	$145	$1,740
Marketing/advertising	$245	$2,940
Services fees/vendors	$60	$720
Marketing support	$110	$1,320
Donations	$60	$720
Auto repairs	$100	$1,200
Client gifts and promotons	$100	$1,200
Virtual assistant support	$125	$1,500
Totals	**$6,428**	**$77,136**
Add 10% for spread and round annual total to nearest $1,000 for ease		
Business Overhead Costs (BOC) total	**$7,085**	**$85,000**

An up-to-date and robust Profit & Loss statement can make this assessment much easier—but don't cheat and pull last year's numbers! As with the personal financial exercises, be as real as you can, and when in doubt, overestimate.

Then, add 10 percent for "spread" since costs for goods, shipping, and other "costs of goods sold" can fluctuate greatly within the span of a year.

Once you've gotten your average monthly costs figured out, multiply them by twelve to get your yearly Business Overhead Cost (or BOC). I've duplicated Rhonda Miller's spreadsheet as an example:

However, as you can see from the chart, Rhonda's basic business overhead looks like this: Fixed/recurring monthly business expenses are $3,107/month, or $37,284/year. However, when we broke down her other business spending and future planned expenses, those added another $3,321, or $39,852 a year! When we added those numbers, we saw that the business needed to produce $77,000 each year to cover overhead costs. And, since I always suggest adding 10 percent to your totals to account for price increases and inflation, we ended up with a final number of $85,000 in overhead costs.

Know Your Numbers

Business Overhead Cost (BOC) = Total recurring and non-recurring expenses required to operate your business

That total of $85,000 (or approximately $7,085 per month) is what the business *must* create in order to break even. Note that this number does not include a salary for Rhonda, or tax expenses.

Good to know, right?

The Whole Picture

Now, let's look at the marriage between your lifestyle and your business.

The amount of revenue your business needs to generate *minus income coming into household* (not your biz income) to maintain your current lifestyle is your Minimum Lifestyle Cost plus your Business Overhead Cost.

For the Millers, that number was:

Minimum Lifestyle cost:	$95,000
Business Overhead Cost:	$85,000
Total Gross Revenue Req.	**$180,000**

Jeff's take-home pay of $53,451 per year means that Rhonda's business needs to generate the shortfall of $106,549 (or approximately $8,900/month) for them to maintain their current lifestyle.

But, let's not forget taxes.

If Rhonda wants to net $106,549 per year, and she and Jeff are in a 22 percent tax bracket (combined Federal/State), that needs to be factored in as well. Some of those taxes will be taken out of Jeff's salary, but most will not. So, to break even, Rhonda's business actually needs to generate a total of approximately $129,000 per year or $10,750 per month.

This number—the minimum amount the business *needs* to generate in order for you to maintain your current lifestyle—is your first Guidepost to creating financial flow and freedom in your life and business. The Guideposts are markers along the way to living and funding your dream life, and each represents a new financial goal.

We'll explore all five Guideposts in depth in Chapter 7—but for now, know that Guidepost #1 (the minimum number you need to generate in order to maintain your current lifestyle) is the *most important number* to know as you move forward to the next stage of the Flow Pillar. Why? Because no matter what else you desire to create for your life and business, you *cannot* shoot below this figure without making changes to your current lifestyle.

Maybe you looked at your total gross revenue requirement and thought, "Easy-peasy. I'm already doing way beyond that!" If that's the case, great.

If you looked at that Guidepost #1 number and thought, "Oh, shit!" that's great, too.

Because now that you know, you can *flow*.

But hey, let's not stop there. We're entrepreneurs, after all. We specialize in big, audacious dreams.

That's why, in Chapter 7, we're going to get the numbers on your biggest goals and create not one but *four* more income guideposts for your business—and demonstrate just how close your dream life might actually be.

But first, let's figure out what that dream life of yours will actually cost.

CHAPTER 6

Level Up to the Dream

WHEN I FOUND OUT that my daughter was pregnant, I identified that a huge goal for me was to be present for the birth of my grandson (one-year goal), but also to visit every six weeks after the baby was born (ten-plus-year goal). We lived in different states—still do—and I was *not* going to be an absentee Gigi! Yes, FaceTime is great, but I wanted real, physical connection—and that required travel.

With 13 hours of drive time between us, I knew I'd have to fly to achieve my every-six-weeks visiting goal. I could stay with my daughter and her husband, as they have an extra bedroom, so I wouldn't have to pay for a hotel, but all those plane tickets were going to add up fast. I needed to know precisely what they were going to cost, and what miles, incentives, and other programs might be available to reduce that cost. After some research, I determined that the one-year cost for those flights would be around $2,844 (nine trips, multiplied by an average economy class ticket cost of $316). I wrote that number in my journal next to my goal, and added it to my "travel expenses" line on my Minimum Lifestyle Cost spreadsheet.

However, I also like to work while I travel, and that's not always comfortable when the person next to me is hogging the armrest and I'm craning my neck at a crazy angle to see my screen. Since this exercise was about creating what I really wanted (as opposed to what I believed, at that moment, was possible for me to have), I gave myself space to explore. What would the cost be for comfortable travel where I could work in the air? And would that extra cost be aligned with my core value of freedom (working anytime, anywhere) and my core value of self-care (working without my body aching and screaming, "Get me *off* this plane!")?

I did some more digging and discovered that the average cost for first-class flights was $820. This meant an annual budget of $7,380 (versus the $2,844 for economy). I added that number to my goal journal and spreadsheet as well.

This was great information to have—but I wasn't finished. There were other costs to my goal besides money. I wanted to be really present for my family while I was visiting. Therefore, I would need to layer in days for travel, and also days where I was "work-free" so I could give my grandchild my full attention. By considering the "time cost" beforehand, I could plan for it and make it a priority, instead of trying to fit things in around the demands of my business. This would mean structuring my client work and programs in a way that allowed me to take chunks of time away from my desk.

As I researched, I envisioned it *all*. The support I'd give my daughter once the baby was born. Truly being there for her, and for the baby, in all the ways I'd fallen short when she was little herself. Rocking the baby to sleep. Bath times. Story times. Holidays, birthdays, and just-because days. My eyes filled with tears at the sheer beauty of it.

My vision and values allowed me to feel into what I wanted—but knowing the cost of my goals helped me figure out the path. I knew how much to add to my travel account each month, and where I needed to reduce expenses to be able to afford my first-class flights. When I put my focus on funding for my first-class tickets, the money started showing up.

Right after my next business trip, one of my airline partners bumped me up to Gold status, which allowed me to upgrade to first class for a mere 500 points/miles. I also partnered with a travel concierge who focused on airline fare specials; over the next few months, I gave her my travel dates and she was able to find first- and business-class flights for significantly under my original budget. None of this would have been possible if I hadn't first seen it as part of my vision and then *believed* it.

And the best part was, when my grandson Carson was born, I was right there beside my daughter, fully present and available to support her, just as I'd promised I would be.

Since then, I've used simple exercises like these to price out regular self-care practices (massage, facials, pedicures), hiring a personal trainer, hiring a private chef to deliver meals for holidays and larger family gatherings, and so much more. These amenities weren't always part of my bottom line, but they are part of my dream life. I know exactly how much they cost, and I design my personal and business financial structures to accommodate those costs. And guess what? None of them were as far out of reach as I previously imagined.

We can't set the GPS until we choose where we're going—and your vision is the *ultimate* destination. That's why, in this chapter, we're going to put price tags on your biggest dreams, your most audacious goals, and your deepest desires.

I've said it before, and I'll say it again: the vision activates the money. The clearer we are about the personal reality we wish to inhabit, the easier it becomes to make choices and commitments that align with and support that reality.

I've heard the argument that pricing your vision gets in the way of manifesting it. I'm going to call bullshit on that one. When you are precise and clear in your asks and are willing to do the work to align yourself with what you desire, God/ Source/the Universe *will* deliver. I would never recommend that you give up your manifestation practice or stop calling in energetic support. However, please don't use Law of Attraction mystery teachings as an excuse to avoid getting clear. In my experience, the only time manifestation *doesn't* work is when you don't know the value of what you're asking for.

If you're tempted to toss out these exercises because your business doesn't (yet) have the money flow to support your goals, don't. The work we will do in this chapter is every bit as important as the work we did in Chapter 5. You may not be able to see the "how" of it all yet, but we'll get there, together. Just keep seeing and claiming your vision.

Let's go.

Next Level LifeStyle Design

How much does your vision *actually* cost?

If you're like most people, you've never done the math to find out how much money it will actually take to fund your biggest dreams and desires. It's one thing to dream and wish, and another to put dates and numbers around those dreams. However, this level of attention and planning is how we bring vision into reality.

Before we begin this process, get out your journal and turn to the goals you set in Chapter 3—particularly your one-year and three-year goals. Then, get out the spreadsheet or list you created in Chapter 5 for your Minimum Lifestyle Costs (MLC).

You will notice that your goals mostly fall into two categories: "stuff" and "experiences." We'll work on the "stuff" first.

In your journal or on your spreadsheet, create a new column next to each of the MLC lifestyle categories, and label it "Minimum Dream Lifestyle Cost" (or just "MDLC")." Plug the items from your goals list into the categories where they belong. Some fun and inspiring examples are included below:

- *Housing expenses.* The monthly mortgage on your dream home. Installing a pool and/or hot tub. Renovating your kitchen. Refinishing the floors. Building a shed or barn.
- *Real estate and investments.* Passive income/rental properties. Flipping houses. International property investments. Starting your own B&B.

- *Debt repayments.* Ideal amounts per month to repay your debt as quickly as possible. What would it cost to pay off your mortgage? Your car? Figure out your time frame.

- *Seasonal purchases.* Hiring a landscaper. Installing a koi pond. Cutting trails through your land. Becoming *the* house to see for Christmas lights in your neighborhood.

- *Transportation expenses.* Your dream car (and associated car payment). Hired cars. Building that garage. Buying a new bike.

- *Food and household items.* Meal preparation. All-organic groceries. Catering for family parties. New sheets, towels, and rugs for your home. That amazing piece of art.

- *Clothing and accessories.* Those shoes with the red soles. That fancy watch. Silk pajamas. A designer purse. Cashmere. Investment and statement pieces. Eco-friendly. Small-designer. B Corp.

- *Medical, dental, vision, and health.* Getting braces, veneers, or capping your teeth. High-end sunglasses. Recovering from surgery in a hotel room. A membership at your yoga studio. A robust Health Savings Account (HSA).

- *Personal expenses & spending money.* An appointment at that upscale salon. Top-end facial and body care products. Bi-weekly manicures and pedicures. Monthly or weekly bodywork, facials, and spa treatments. Specialized healing treatments. Yearly membership at the yacht club or golf course.

- *Travel.* Living abroad for a season. First-class tickets for every trip. Five-star accommodations. Buying a boat, or RV. Working from anywhere.

- *Kids' expenses.* A fully-funded college savings account. Semesters abroad. Inviting friends on family vacations. More time together.

- *Pets.* Buying that special breed. Building a horse barn (and buying a horse). Traveling with pets.

- *Gifts.* Sharing your abundance with family and friends. Leaving random $100 tips. Buying Mom a new car. Paying for your nephew's summer camp.

- *Charity/donations.* Supporting individuals or businesses on a higher level. Funding charity trips. Donating a building to your college. Saving your local library.

- *Savings.* Ideal contributions to 401k, IRAs, non-qualified accounts, and other retirement accounts. Ideal emergency fund and savings account balances. Early retirement.

- *Miscellaneous.* Your imagination is the limit here!

- *Future planned spending:* What lives beyond your biggest vision? Price that out, too!*

Now, start doing your research. What is the price of every item on your list? Add those dollar amounts to your spreadsheet, making sure to estimate on the high end and include sales tax, shipping, installation, and other associated costs.

---

* Go to www.MichelleJacobik.com/PathtoProfitsResources to download interactive spreadsheets!

Once you're finished with the "stuff," it's time to move on to the experiential goals. For example, if you have a goal to lose twenty pounds and regain your energy, what will that cost? Will you need to hire a personal trainer, a nutritionist, or a coach? Will you need to invest in supplements, organic produce, or new running shoes?

Or, maybe you have a goal to retire at fifty-five. What exactly will you need to have in the bank to make that happen? How much will you need to save/invest each month from now until then? Do you need to hire an accountant, financial planner, or wealth manager?

Not all experiential goals will require an investment—but a surprising number of them will. Even a goal like "be more present with my kids" might be easier to attain with strategic spending—like a personal assistant to pick up groceries and dry cleaning so you can spend fewer hours running around. Again, let your imagination roam free. This is about your dreams and vision, not your current reality.

Once you've estimated costs for all of your one- and three-year goals, get out your calculator and add it all up. Then, subtract your current non-business income flow (the same number you used to generate your MLC in Chapter 5). What you'll end up with is your Minimum Dream Lifestyle Cost, or MDLC.

What is the actual difference between your current MLC and your MDLC? More importantly, what does it feel like to know *exactly* how many dollars per year it will take to create a life that is fully aligned with your core values, your vision, your desires, and your big dreams? Don't let the numbers scare you. Remember, in order to *flow*, you have to *know!*

Next-Level Business Design

Now that we know what your dream life will actually cost, it's time to take your business numbers to the next level, too. As we did for your personal finances, we will build on your numbers and notes from the Business Overhead Cost (BOC) exercise in Chapter 5.

Imagine that your business is thriving in excess of your wildest expectations. What will that look like? Who will you hire, and what will you pay them? What expenses will be added, and which will stay the same? Which will go away entirely?

Doing these projections will give you what I call your Business Vision Overhead Cost (BVOC)—meaning, the approximate cost associated with fully realizing your big vision—and show you the financial gap between your current business and your dream business.

So, get out your BOC/cash flow spreadsheet from Chapter 5, and add new line items under the heading "BVOC." How will these dream business operating costs affect your monthly cash flow? What dream business operating costs need to be considered in each of the following categories?

- *Employee expenses.* Whom do you need to hire, and at what salary? What benefits packages do you plan to add? Add up yearly salaries and benefits costs and divide by twelve to get your average monthly expenses.

- *Physical location.* Are you buying a building? Moving to a bigger location? Renovating or adding an addition?

- *Insurance.* How will your insurance needs change? What additional coverages will you require?

- *Transportation and shipping.* Will you be adding additional vehicles? Increasing travel for yourself or your employees? Hosting events?

- *Equipment.* What do you need to buy/lease/repair?

- *Banking and credit cards.* How will increasing your revenue impact credit card processing fees, credit card interest payments, bank fees, lines of credit, etc.?

- *Utilities.* What will you need to add or improve in terms of phone systems, alarm systems, cell phone and data bills, internet, etc.?

- *Subscriptions.* How will expansion affect your tech stack? Also consider additional or upgraded association dues and subscriptions, networking memberships, etc.

- *Production of goods, packaging, and shipping.* What is the cost to add products to your existing SKUs, move from holding inventory to drop-shipping, hire a co-packer, or engage a fulfillment company to do the work for you?

- *Accounting and legal.* What financial or legal processes need to be created or adapted? What about trademarking costs, updated contracts, or liability waivers? What would it cost to bring on a fractional (part-time) financial manager or full-time CFO?

- *Future planned expenses.* Add any "good to have" items that, while not truly necessary, would make your expansion smoother, easier, or just more fun!

- *Tax expenses.* With bigger revenues comes a bigger tax bill. Plan for it!*

Just like in Chapter 5, estimate your average monthly costs, then multiply by twelve to get your yearly Business Vision Overhead Cost. Don't forget to add an additional 10 percent for spread!

Chances are, this number will feel *really* big. That's okay, because we are going to chunk it down into manageable steps in Chapter 7.

Even though I'm a financial expert, I love to keep things simple in my life and business. For me, that means doing things in a certain order. This helps me feel "goal-focused" and also helps me communicate better with my husband Jody, my team, and my clients. When I have a clear blueprint, I also make better decisions about which opportunities to jump on and which to save for a more appropriate time.

So, go back to the itemized expenses for your BVOC. Which of these expenses will be incurred in the first twelve months? Which in the first three years? Which in the first five years? Which will increase gradually with time (such as payroll, production costs, taxes, etc.), and which will require one large sum (such as equipment or real estate purchases)?

With your trusty calculator and a little creative thinking, you will soon have not only your BVOC for your ultimate dream business, but also stepping stones to get you there. Hooray!

---

* Go to www.MichelleJacobik.com/PathtoProfitsResources to download interactive spreadsheets!

Look Your Business in the Face

What I love most about the Flow Pillar of the EnVision process is that it helps entrepreneurs get off the fence and get to work. Seeing clearly what a profitable business can do for them has snapped hundreds of my clients out of analysis paralysis. With their MDLC and BVOC numbers in front of them, they can clearly see the costs of following influencers and industry experts down rabbit holes, overinvesting in unnecessary tech, or pouring resources into unprofitable offers. With their biggest visions mapped out dollar by dollar, they can confidently spend their time on revenue-generating activities that will make the cash register ring!

However, there's another side to this process, and it's one that many people will go miles out of their way to avoid. When you go through the Flow Pillar, you will be forced to look your business in the face—and you may not like what you see.

If you've been running your business on hope and credit, you probably just got a harsh wake-up call. If your financial goals require more work from you than there are hours in the day, you may have just realized that your current business model isn't capable of taking you where you want to go. I know it's hard—but burying your head in the sand isn't the answer. If you keep doing that, you will contribute another percentage point to the "failed businesses" statistic.

If you ignore your numbers, *you will kill your business.* Maybe not today, or tomorrow, or even next year. But eventually, your business will collapse—either because you can no longer ride the financial rollercoaster, or because you failed to plan for unavoidable change.

I don't want you to fail. I want you to *win*. I want to flip the statistics and empower the majority of businesses to succeed beyond their owners' wildest dreams. More than that, I want *you* to fully realize those big, audacious dreams of yours. I want you to succeed to the point where you can change not only your own life, but the lives of everyone around you.

So, if seeing your MDLC or BVOC numbers felt scary, frustrating, or just plain impossible, just remember: there is *always* a way forward. What you'll learn in Chapter 7 will help you create a solid financial foundation and establish goal posts along the journey. We'll talk about the where, when, and how of your big vision, and explore how to evolve your business if it isn't capable of supporting your vision in its current form.

So please, even if you're not sure how the heck it will all play out, do the work. Look at the whole picture. Feel the fear and *do it anyway*, because your dream life is waiting.

CHAPTER 7
Guideposts

MARY AND I STARTED working together almost two decades ago, when I was still in the insurance business. I was her insurance advisor for more than ten years—right up until I sold my portion of that business. A few years later, we reconnected when she and her husband attended my Financial Peace University class. She and her husband, Tim, were both entrepreneurs—she owned a sports academy and he was a plumber—and they were looking for creative ways to get out of debt and move closer to their dream of owning their own sports facility.

To say Mary was an eager student would be a serious understatement. We also had a lot of mutual trust from our previous business relationship. She jokingly told the class, "I told Tim that if he listens to the pretty lady at the front of the room, he might get something out of this … and if not, he still gets to listen to the pretty lady at the front of the room!"

"Way to make me blush," I replied.

Tim, true to his word, listened quietly throughout the presentation. Mary not only listened but also took copious notes, filling every white space in the workbook. Later, she told me, "I made a decision that day. I decided that I was ready. More than that, I was willing—willing to do whatever it took to turn our financial situation around and hit my big goals."

Her determination was incredibly inspiring—and she would need every last bit of it. You see, Mary knew that it would cost her over $2,300,000 to construct the building she dreamed of and expand her business to include management of the facility. She had already been "crowdfunding" for ten years with her family of customers, selling tiles, hosting fundraisers, and asking for support from every quarter. But getting a bank to say yes to a note that size was going to take more than just passion. She would need strong financials and a personal guarantee from both her and Tim. Add to that the land purchase of about $150,000, which she intended to do in cash, and a down payment of nearly $200,000 on the massive construction loan, and … well, it was a *lot* of money.

The financial pistons required to scale a business using bank or investor leverage are far beyond opening a business as a solopreneur or making calculated small moves to grow an existing model. I remembered being there when I bought my share of my insurance business. Cash, leverage, good credit, collateral, personal guarantees, and good strong numbers were musts. I had to prove that I had what it took to manage the repayment terms of $15,000 to $17,000 per month, in addition to all our other operating expenses.

To Mary, this was the Big Dream, and she knew it would require not only clear vision but a hefty dose of trust—both in herself and in the business model she'd designed. She knew she couldn't dream her way into position for something on this scale. She had to be intentional and make the right moves— both when it came to getting a yes from the bank, but also when it came to running this new, expanded version of her business after making the big leap. So, we developed a three-year plan for both her personal finances and her business to help her put her money in the right places and enter into these big negotiations with confidence.

What's Your Growth Plan?

If you're anything like Mary, your big vision—for your personal life and for your business—will require a lot more capital than your business is currently generating. And, since you did the exercises in Chapter 5 and Chapter 6, you now know *exactly* how much your business is currently generating, how much it needs to generate in order to sustain both itself and you, and how much extra is required to create your vision!

Bridging the gap between where you are and where you're going will not only require you to set big goals, but also to clean up the skeletons in your financial closet, since they will *all* be on display when you either a) ask for money, or b) go through a business expansion that changes your financial reality. In order to thrive through massive growth and avoid the crash and burn, you need to be positioned in healthy ways in your business and your personal finances.

For example, if, like Mary, you desire to buy or build a massive commercial property, will your business need that extra $10,000 a month you may have been taking as a paycheck to pay the mortgage until you finish construction? How will that look for your LifeStyle Design? Before you take that pay cut, will you need to clean up that lingering credit card debt to reduce your monthly expenses, pay off your car loan, or consolidate your credit card debt?

Or maybe your planned expansion requires you to hire one, or two, or several employees. Since their salaries will now take priority, will you be able to sustain your business's bottom line until revenues catch up?

In order to get to where you want to go, you may need to do things differently than you have previously done them. It takes serious financial chops to get strategic around your big dreams and say no to all the glossy, intriguing opportunities that will come your way. However, making those strategic decisions gets easier when you have the hard numbers!

That's why I've created the Path to Profits Guideposts. They are the milestones for your business that I believe every entrepreneur *must* hit in order to create a solid financial foundation to support their dream life.

These Guideposts are not "fluffy" goals or aspirations. They are *real* income goals for your business that will empower you to create your dream lifestyle.

The Path to Profit Guideposts are:

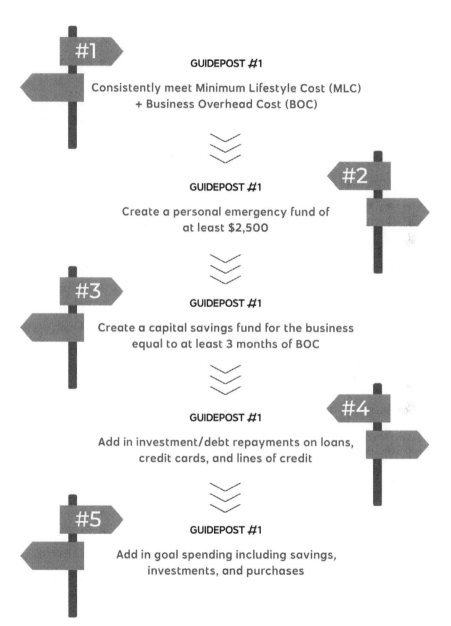

GUIDEPOST #1

Consistently meet Minimum Lifestyle Cost (MLC)
+ Business Overhead Cost (BOC)

GUIDEPOST #1

Create a personal emergency fund of
at least $2,500

GUIDEPOST #1

Create a capital savings fund for the business
equal to at least 3 months of BOC

GUIDEPOST #1

Add in investment/debt repayments on loans,
credit cards, and lines of credit

GUIDEPOST #1

Add in goal spending including savings,
investments, and purchases

You'll notice that your goal items don't appear until Guidepost #5. There's a good reason for that. When you have Guideposts #1 through #4 in place, you and your business will be far more capable of initiating and sustaining strategic growth (and staying on the winning side of those "business success" statistics).

Let's look at the Guideposts in more depth. Once again, I'll use the Millers as an illustrative example.

Guidepost #1: Cover your business overhead and personal lifestyle

Remember, your MLC and BOC are the absolute minimum amounts you must create in order to sustain yourself at your current lifestyle level. If, after doing the exercises in Chapter 5, you found yourself coming up short of these numbers, it's time for a business triage. I strongly advise against moving forward with any of the rest of the Guideposts until you plug this hole and stop the financial bleeding.

If you recall, for Rhonda and Jeff Miller that number was $180,000—$95,000 for MLC, $85,000 for BOC. Since Jeff's take-home pay was $53,451 per year, Rhonda's business needed to generate at least $106,549 to maintain their lifestyle.

Guidepost #1
Annual income goal: MLC + BOC

Guidepost #2: Create a "baby" personal emergency fund of $2,500

At the time of writing, the world is beginning to emerge from the depths of a global pandemic. During the two-year period between 2020 and 2022, I watched many businesses crumble. Lockdowns, restructuring, and the Great Resignation wreaked havoc on small businesses everywhere.

During the pandemic, many initiatives were put in place to support businesses and business owners. For the first time, entrepreneurs were eligible for unemployment benefits. Paycheck Protection Program (PPP) loans, stimulus checks, and other support structures were lifelines for millions of people. However, many of those programs didn't kick in until months after the lockdowns began—which was, in many cases, too late.

An emergency fund isn't a luxury. It's a necessity. It's insurance against the challenges that none of us can predict. Before you start building your vision, tuck some cash away so you don't have to give up on your dreams when you hit a bump (or a tanker-sized sinkhole) in the financial road.

Guidepost #2
Annual income goal: MLC + BOC + $2,500

Guidepost #3: Create a Capital Savings Fund (CSF) for your business that includes at least three to six months of total operating expenses (including your salary).

What your emergency fund is for you personally, your Capital Savings Fund is for your business.

Could your business survive if you had a month with no sales? For many entrepreneurs, the answer to that question is, "Not a chance." Before you move on to Guidepost #4, set aside enough cash to pay all your operating costs (including your own salary and those of your team) for at least three months. This is your Capital Savings Fund, or CSF.

This one Guidepost could literally be the deciding factor in the survival of your business.

Because we already know Rhonda and Jeff Miller's annual MLC and BOC, we can easily figure out the ideal amount for their CSF. We simply take that total number from Guidepost #1 ($180,000), divide it by twelve to get an average monthly total ($15,000), and then multiply by the number of months (three or six) that they have decided will create an ideal level of stability and insulation. Rhonda and Jeff decided that they were comfortable with three months as they had established both a personal home equity line as well as a business line of credit that they could access in a worst-case scenario. So, their CSF should equal at least $45,000 (including the $2,500 emergency fund they established in Guidepost #2). This adjusted their total annual income goal for Rhonda's business to $151,549.

Guidepost #3
Annual income goal: MLC + BOC + CSF

Guidepost #4: Add in investment/debt repayments on loans, credit cards, and lines of credit to both MLC and BOC

Now that you have a nice cushion for both you and your business, it's time to start paying down debt. I know it's not sexy or exciting, but trying to build wealth while you still have debt is like building your dream house on a sand dune.

However, there's a caveat. You can do this at your own pace.

At this point, you've created relative financial security for yourself and your business. With your emergency accounts funded, you should have some extra money each month to play with. You can throw it all at your debt (using Dave Ramsey's 'Debt Snowball' method or another debt-erasing plan), or you can take a more moderate approach. The latter option will allow you to start putting money toward your vision and goals, funding your retirement plans, or expanding your business at the same time as you're paying down your debt.

The balance you strike here is up to you. If you are younger, you may choose to throw everything you have at your debt so you can create greater financial freedom later. If you are older, funding your retirement accounts might feel more important than paying off your mortgage or student loans. Or maybe you're dedicated to living your best life, and you're happy making just over the minimum payments on your debt while investing in the things that make life feel exciting and rich.

The Millers chose to set a goal of paying off their $14,000 in credit card debt, $34,000 car loan balance, and $47,000 in lingering student loan debt. After much discussion around the big picture, they set a goal of having all these debts paid within five years. The total of these was $96,000, so we divided that by five ($19,200) and added that number to their Guidepost #3 number to get their Guidepost #4 income goal of $170,749.

The one hard and fast guideline is this: don't ignore your debt; and, unless you're making a strategic investment like Mary's land and building purchase, try not to add to it.

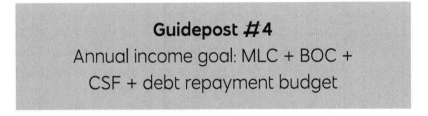

Guidepost #4
Annual income goal: MLC + BOC +
CSF + debt repayment budget

Guidepost #5: Add in goal spending to both MLC and BOC, including lifestyle stuff/experience expenses, retirement savings, etc.

Here's where things get really fun. When you reach this Guidepost, it's time to start funding your dreams.

Revisit the work you did in the last chapter. What was your total Minimum Dream Lifestyle Cost (MDLC) and your total Business Vision Operating Cost (BVOC)? Bring in those numbers here.

Now, choose the most important and amazing line items from those lists. What would make your life more exciting, streamlined, or luxurious *right now?* Pull out those items and add them up. (You don't need to include everything on your MDLC and BVOC right now—we are focused on the items that coincide with your one- and three-year goals.)

If you feel like those numbers are way too big, please don't back away now! You've come this far, and if you're going to build your dream life, you may as well shoot for what you truly desire! Why go to the playoffs when you can land yourself in the Superbowl?

Now, you don't have to try to hit this final income goal all at once. However, with every dollar you create over your Guidepost #4 total, you can begin to bring in aspects of your dream life and business!

Remember the Millers from Chapter 5? Here's how they designed their "Superbowl win":

We added four vacations (total: $20,000), retirement savings ($15,000), a part-time assistant ($20,800), social media support ($5,400), and a mother's helper ($15,600) who could take over laundry, meal prep, and running the kids to and from lessons. The total for these upgrades was $76,800. So, Rhonda's Guidepost #5 income goal for her business came in at $247,549.

By this point, you are super clear. These Guideposts are simply a way of positioning your dollars in advance. I call this "ordering it up" from myself and the Universe.

Get excited, my friend. It's all arriving.

> ### **Guidepost #5**
> Annual income goal: MLC + BOC +
> CSF + debt repayment budget + one-
> year goal MDLC/BVOC items

Accounting is Accountability

You can't make long-term decisions while you're drowning.

In the same way, you can't understand the root cause of problems (or successes) in your business if the facts are clouded by your emotions and biases. The numbers you've accessed in the Flow Pillar can help you see things as they truly are.

Accounting is accountability. Used in the right ways, it can help you march toward your mission, achieve your vision, and build your legacy. This is why accounting needs to be part of your daily business functions—and by "accounting" I don't just mean sending invoices and collecting checks. I mean tracking, assessing, and forecasting.

The numbers in your business separate the signals from the noise. They can show you when things are going well and teach you how to expand them, and also where things are going wrong and where you need to correct them.

The Flow Pillar of the EnVision process is, at its heart, about moving you and your business away from "bank balance" accounting and into a stronger, more empowering model of operational financial management.

Let me explain:

Bank balance accounting is the most primitive form of business accounting. Typically conducted in spreadsheets or a basic bookkeeping app, you tally all your expenses and income from your bank statements once a quarter (or once a year, at tax time). What makes this method popular among new business owners is that it's cheap, easy, and relatively simple to do. However, while it is a solution to filing your taxes, it is not a viable tool to proactively manage your Path to Profits.

My recommendation is to get away from this simplified form of accounting as soon as possible and lean into a cash flow planning system that allows you to make clear operational decisions in your business. You may have thought this level of financial management was only for the big dogs—but after working through the Flow Pillar, you're already more than halfway there!

Operating costs	Jan	Feb	Mar	Apr	May	June	July	Aug	Sept	Oct	Nov	Dec
Current monthly bills including credit card minimums, utilities, rent												
Gas												
Supplies and shipping												
Listing expenses												
Conferences/travel												
Dues, subscriptions, insurance												
Training and education												
Annual retreat/summit												
Networking connectioions												
Networking events												
Marketing/advertising												
Services fees/vendors												
Marketing support												
Donations												
Auto repairs												
Client gifts and promotons												
Virtual assistant support												
Totals												
Add 10% for spread and round annual total to nearest $1,000 for ease												
Business Overhead Costs (BOC) total												

You already have the current BOC and BVOC numbers for your business. Now, we can take those and leverage them to create a twelve- to thirty-six-month forecasting view. This will give you not only a clear picture of where your money is going, but where it needs to go in the future to accomplish your goals and meet upcoming obligations.

In the spreadsheet opposite, you'll see how this works. The expenses are listed in rows down the left-hand side and broken out month by month across the columns. The year-to-date totals are tallied in the right-hand column. Using this model, you can either spread upcoming expenses evenly across the coming months (so you are budgeting the funds in advance), or allocate them to the months when they will occur.

For examples, my insurance license (which I still maintain) renews every two years. My business insurances—like Workers' Compensation, Business Owners Insurance, Professional Liability, and event coverages—renew once a year. All are due in full in the month of September. So, on my forecasting spreadsheet, I can either allocate a set amount each month to prepare and save for those payments, or I can drop the entire amount in the September column so I'm not surprised when the bill arrives.

ALLOCATION TIPS

You may be wondering, "How do I tell my money where to go in advance when it's all in one business checking account?"

I actually encourage my clients to have multiple bank accounts for their businesses, and for their personal finances as well. You can open as many accounts as you think will be helpful, but here are some to start with:

- *Operating Account.* This is a checking account where all your income will arrive, and where all monthly recurring bills and overheads that are not noted in the "forecasted" or "pre-saving" columns are paid from.

- *Future Planned Expenses Account.* This is a checking account where you will keep the funds being budgeted for things that are not due yet. I suggest moving these funds from your Operating Account to this one once a month, and then using a virtual envelope app to divide those deposits into categories so you know exactly what that lump sum is for.

- *Tax Account.* This is a savings account where tax deposits are held monthly or quarterly until due again. On the tenth day of the month (after your bookkeeper has reconciled everything from the previous month), move the anticipated tax liability based on your net profits into this account and *do not touch it.* (If you are disciplined, you could forego this separate account and simply create a virtual envelope category within your Future Planned Expenses account.

- *Capital Savings Account.* This is a money market or savings account you can easily access when needed. (Again, if you are disciplined, you could forego this account and simply create a virtual envelope category for your Capital Savings Funds. However, if you are planning to save three to six months of expenses for Guidepost #3, it's helpful to have those funds in an interest-producing account.)

Splitting up your funds in this way helps you shift from looking only at your checking account balance on a daily basis and thinking, "As long as there is enough money in there to pay the bills this week, I'm good."

When we are able to see a twelve-month outward view (what I call your Allocated Cash Flow View) of your budgeted expenses spread across your spreadsheets, bank accounts, and virtual envelopes, you will consciously and subconsciously become more aware of weighing risks, not overspending, and seeing how decisions will impact all areas of your business. When you drop in your anticipated income for each month at the top of the spreadsheet, you will easily see where you require more income or a cash injection. You will know precisely what your business needs to generate for profits to meet your current Guidepost, and also what revenue generation strategy will most easily help you meet your next income goal.

SUPPORT FOR YOUR FLOW PILLAR

As a business owner, you need to be spending your time on high-leverage activities. So, unless you truly love numbers and have a strong background in the financial realms, you'll want to call in support to streamline your Flow Pillar processes and help you keep your eyes on what really matters: your vision and your numbers.

Below are some people you'll want to call in to your business sphere to support you as you move through your Guideposts.

- *A great bookkeeper.* Most business owners perceive bookkeeping as a commoditized administrative function—a compliance activity that makes their lives easier on tax day but otherwise has little value. This is a deadly misconception. Your bookkeeper is one of the most valuable players in your business as they support the financial function of your entire organization. A good bookkeeper can fulfill this role until you grow to about $250,000 in annual revenue.

- *A financial manager or fractional/part-time CFO.* After your business reaches the $250,000/year range, consider upgrading to a financial manager or fractional/part-time CFO who can help you lean into more analysis and strategy to ensure your financial health. I play this role with many of my private consultancy clients; together, we move from bank balance accounting to operational finance, build forecasting and predictive reporting processes, and develop a rolling budget. For many entrepreneurs, this is the missing link. Having this information can help you deal with funding mechanisms, pricing, raising capital, applying for loans, mergers and acquisitions, and long-term shareholder creation. If you aim to be a "big" business, a strategic financial manager is worth their weight in gold.

- *A Certified Public Accountant (CPA).* Hiring an accredited tax professional to ensure you are filing your taxes properly is good business. Having a tax professional who will advise you throughout the year on how you can lower your tax liability is *great* business!

- *A financial board of advisors.* In addition to your bookkeeper and/or financial manager and your CPA, you will want to expand your financial team to include an experienced business consultant like me, a trusted attorney, an insurance professional, and an investment/wealth advisor as early as possible. This team is key to making, protecting, and keeping more money and, in turn, activating your financial freedom. They should all know about each other (yes, please introduce them!) so they can work as a team to support your long-term success.

Behind all the most successful businesses and individuals is a team of financial professionals. Asking for support does not mean you can't handle your money; rather, it means that you're committed to treating your money as the critically-important resource it is!

Alignment Always Comes First

At this point in our work together, you should know exactly how much money is flowing in and out of your accounts each month, and what you need to be making to both sustain your lifestyle and grow into your vision.

But before we move forward into the Grow Pillar, there are other, deeper questions that need to be answered, such as:

- "Is my business model actually aligned with my desired lifestyle?"
- "Is my business capable of scaling to produce the level of personal income that I desire?"
- "Am I truly willing to do what it takes to make this happen—and is that level of effort aligned with my values and vision?"

You may have already started asking these kinds of questions in the Vision Pillar, when we looked at how your core values align with your business and work flow. Now, we need to ask them from the money side.

A business that cannot support the life you desire and deserve is not a business you should be in. Period. That might be hard to hear right now, but it is the absolute truth. You're not in business to be a servant to your business. You're in business to support your life. If that's not happening, something needs to shift.

To determine whether your business is aligned with your vision, journal on the following questions:

- "Is my business currently producing the amount of cash flow necessary to meet my MLC and BOC? If not, what will it take to get it to the point where it is producing at that level?"

- "Is my business scalable to the point that it can support my MDLC and BVOC? What will I need to do to achieve that?"

And, most importantly:

- "Are the actions I will need to get my business producing at the levels required by my dream life aligned with, or contradictory to, my core values and the life I truly desire?"

When we start asking questions about cash flow and scaling, the normal response from most entrepreneurs is, "I'll just work harder." That's fine—*if* your desired lifestyle and core values support that approach. But if your entire vision is about slowing down, family, self-care, time freedom, travel, etc., be careful of saying, "I'll just do it for a little while." (Remember my Sunday night webinars? Seriously, don't do that.)

Nothing is more important than your quality of life. Not even your business. And if you don't prioritize your vision when it comes to scaling your business, you *will* end up frustrated, burned out, and exhausted.

So, if your business isn't supporting your MLC and BOC, your business model needs to change. If you value time with family and friends, yet you can't scale your business without it eating up every second of your free time, your business model needs to change. If you value freedom and yet can't envision your business running without your constant direction and input, your business model needs to change.

Most people come to this stage of the game exhausted, depleted, and just trying to "stay in business" because they don't want to be seen as someone who failed. If that's you, I hear you. I feel you. And it's time to stop hitting yourself over the head with these unhelpful narratives. There is no shame in retiring what is no longer working. This isn't a question of acceptance; it's a question of alignment.

Money is energy, and it can be created in a multitude of ways. The best way to create money is one that is in full alignment with your values. If you can come back to the core truth that you are a creator, you can more easily identify new and different ways to create.

Remember, the EnVision process isn't just about business success, although that's a big part of it. It's really about creating a life you want to be living *and* having a business that supports that.

Surrender isn't looking down in defeat. It's stopping your spinning, putting your back on the earth, and looking *up* for guidance.

So, whether you reinvent, streamline, sell, close, bring on a partner, find a strategic business advisor like me, or just commit to doing things differently, know that this is all in service to who you are and the impact you came here to create.

Your vision is calling you. Let it *flow* so you can *grow.*

PILLAR III
Grow

CHAPTER 8

Growing Your Wings

ON NEW YEAR'S EVE, 2021, while the rest of the world was preparing for their celebratory evenings, I was prepping for a segment on New York's PIX11 4:00 p.m. news. I had originally taken the week off to relax and recharge, but when I was offered the opportunity to share a segment I had pitched to the network six weeks earlier, my response was a full-on "Yes!"

Why would I do that? Why give up my New Year's Eve for a last-minute media opportunity? Isn't that just like giving up my Sundays for webinars?

Well, yes—and no.

This was an aligned decision for me because I knew that saying yes to a producer who needs a "fill-in" when something previously planned falls through goes a long way in television media. Because I know that saying yes to my own visibility and expert status, even on days when I'd planned to take a rest, always lights me up. Because I get to choose when, how, and for whom to move my personal boundaries. And because I know that saying no to that kind of visibility means that fewer people know about my work and my mission to flip entrepreneurial success statistics on their heads—which, in turn, means fewer future opportunities, smaller profits, and harder work for me.

So, instead of relaxing with my hubby and a big glass of white wine, I put on my game face and delivered a segment I was proud of and that got thousands of eyes on my business. Then, I poured that glass of wine and celebrated the hell out of myself.

I've spent most of my career leading and supporting entrepreneurs in one way or another: by insuring them, connecting them, elevating them, and mentoring them. I've watched my clients struggle, strive, and eventually bring their biggest dreams into the world—both those you've met in this book, and many, many more.

But, over and over, I've also witnessed the leaders of companies both small and large bust their butts to get their products and services ready to share with their communities, only to play it small on the visibility front. They assumed that a colorful new window sign, a shoutout from their local Chamber of Commerce, or a few Facebook ads would be enough to magnetize people to their offers. While those pieces can be important, public relations and relationship marketing are ongoing efforts that must be worked into every business's plan. If you want to have long-term growth, continuous sales, increased cash flow, and greater profitability, you need to let people know who you are and what you stand for.

When I bought my first company at the age of twenty-nine, I had zero dollars in my budget for advertising. I had drained my bank accounts and most of my investments, and leveraged every part of my life to purchase the company I worked for. So, I had to get super creative with my advertising plan. I needed to let people know that the ownership had changed, that we were open for business, and that we were hungry for *more.*

More, because I had a payroll with eight people on it. More, because I now had a five-figure loan payable every month for the next fifteen years, and I wanted it gone in seven. More, because I had a mortgage to pay on the house we'd purchased a year earlier, and a little girl who needed to be fed and clothed, not just loved. I wanted more because failure was not an option.

I wouldn't change those early years in the insurance business for anything, because they taught me everything I know about how to get free publicity. I learned to write and send monthly press releases and business briefs. I submitted regular articles on my expert topics to local newspapers and magazines. I landed us on radio spots and interviews and used creative white-space-buying tactics to get advertising for pennies on the dollar. I even convinced the president of the bank to write an article about us, since we were the largest SBA loan they had ever underwritten. They plastered our pictures right on the cover of their glossy mailer that went to every business and depositor on their rosters!

And, most of all, I learned to be consistent with my efforts, so my wins weren't short-lived. Every day, I was thinking about how to keep eyes on our business so our phones would keep ringing.

In the Grow Pillar, we are going to take a deep dive into growing your visibility, expert status, and audience so you can shorten your timeline to success and meet those beautiful Guidepost numbers we fleshed out in the Flow Pillar. We will look at both sides of the growth coin—client attraction and client retention—as well as the mindset pieces necessary to scale your business without burning out.

This is where your business grows its wings.

What, Why, How

Before we can lean into the visibility portion of your plan, we need to know three things:

- What are you striving to create for yourself?
- Why are you the best at what you do?
- What exactly are you selling?

The plans you make in the Grow Pillar will depend largely on the values and goals you identified in the Vision Pillar and the financial goals you identified in the Flow Pillar. If you only need to increase your business revenue by $50,000 to $60,000 to create your vision and live your best life, your plan will look much different than if you want your business to scale from $100,000 to $5 million in annual revenues in three years. Neither is right or wrong—but they will require vastly different strategies.

Second, you absolutely must understand why you are the best person to do what you're doing. Are you better than other players in your field? Are you the best at what you do?

Does that question rub you the wrong way?

I'm not asking you to become an egomaniac. I simply want you to realize that, until you figure out what makes you the best at what you do, you will have a much harder time positioning yourself to stand out from the crowd.

So, grab your journal and a pen, and write, "I am the best in my industry because ..."

Here are a few ideas to get you started:

- "I respond faster than any other provider."
- "I have the best customer service out there."
- "My product is totally fair trade and eco-friendly."
- "I focus on top quality and will do the job until it's done right."
- "I donate 5 percent of my gross profits to charity."
- "I help people create greater impact in their work."
- "I am a genius at helping people clarify their vision and put it to work."
- "My team can solve any logistical issue in under five days."

Get specific with these. The places where you stand out will become the foundation of your visibility efforts. You might not resonate with being "the best" in the whole world—but I know you can find at least three areas where you truly outshine the competition.

BRIDGING THE GAP

I'd be willing to bet that, since the moment you completed the exercises in the Flow Pillar, you've been thinking about how to close the gap between where you are now and where you want to be.

If you haven't done so already, you can get your "Gap" number using this formula.

$$\textit{Guidepost \#5 - Guidepost \#1 = Gap*}$$

Chances are, you already have products and services in place that can close that gap—*if* you can get enough people to buy them. (Or you're designing the products and services that can.)

That's what we will focus on in this chapter. We'll look first at your revenue streams, then your visibility and client attraction strategy, then your strategy for nurturing current clients. When you take the time to do this work, even if it seems repetitive to what you already know and are doing, you will be more likely to implement consistently, and therefore move the needle in your business and on your balance sheet.

YOUR REVENUE STREAMS

How will you close your Gap? Through sales, of course!

Draw a line down the center of a page in your journal. At the top of the left column, write your Guidepost #1 number. At

---

* If your business hasn't yet reached Guidepost #1, use the numbers for where you are now to get an accurate picture.

the top of the right column, write your Guidepost #5 number. Then, in each column, write the name of each of your current offers, products, or services, and how many of each you need to sell to generate the amount for that Guidepost. It might look something like this:

GAP: $150,000

	Guidepost #1	Guidepost #5	Gap amount
Offer #1	# to sell to create Guidepost $	# to sell to create Guidepost $	# of sales to close Gap
Offer #2	# to sell to create Guidepost $	# to sell to create Guidepost $	# of sales to close Gap
Offer #3	# to sell to create Guidepost $	# to sell to create Guidepost $	# of sales to close Gap

If you are in insurance, real estate, or another commission-based sales model, you can rank your "offers" by the amount of commission you will receive. For example, if you're in insurance, you could break out your "offers" into corporate, small businesses, and personal buckets. If you're in real estate, you could break them out into the property value tiers you'd like to focus on.

Now, ask yourself the following questions for each of your columns:

- Who are the buyers of this offer?
- Where do they hang out?
- Who is already serving them?
- What do they need that only I can provide?

Do this until you have a clear picture of the ideal customer/client for each of your current offers. This information will inform every piece of your visibility plan.

Your Visibility Plan

The aim of any business is to make a profit, but there's no profit to be made if no one knows about your business.

Now that we know what you're selling, who you're selling it to, and why you're the best person to sell it, it's time to look at where you can show up and be seen!

The good news is, it doesn't take a lot of time or money to increase visibility for your business. What it does take is consistency, willingness, and the bravery to be both bold and discerning in your marketing efforts. Investing in small but aligned efforts can do a lot more to create a positive impact than cookie-cutter approaches. Instead of throwing spaghetti at the wall (like Angelica from Chapter 3 was doing before we met), ask yourself, "What do I enjoy doing that will make the biggest difference in my visibility right now?"

One note: As we explore avenues for growth, you are going to find things that are authentic to you and your business, and others that aren't. Trust yourself and follow your intuition. However, before you make a decision about whether to use any of the growth strategies I'm about to share, make sure that you are taking the time and using your personal practices (like meditation, journaling, visioning, etc.) to discern whether your "no" is coming from your truth or your fear. I can't tell you how many times a client has told me, "Oh, no. TV/radio/podcasts/

livestreaming are *not* for me," when they were simply afraid of being seen. Once they worked through their fear, most realized that those avenues were *absolutely* aligned for their business, and that they actually loved doing them!

ALL ROADS LEAD TO SALES

In this section we will explore some of the best ways to get more visible in your business. Some of them may be familiar; some may surprise you. Some may be complex, others basic. All of them will require your attention and consistency over a period of time to be fully effective. Rather than try everything at once, start with one or two that light you up. I'll share an exercise around picking your visibility pathways later in this section.

Online Presence

Your business has many online identities: your website, your Google listing, your social media accounts, your YouTube channel, your membership listing in that professional association you joined, your affiliation with your local Chamber of Commerce or virtual networking group. It's truly important that all these represent you, your company, and your brand. I'm not saying go out and rebrand yourself—but chances are, what's out there needs an audit. I can't tell you how many times I've helped clients do this review only to find that their online representation looks nothing like their true business.

When I pivoted from offering divorce support, I had to look under the hood of my online presence. Not only did I need to update my website and blog (which were filled with divorce support articles and links), I also had to examine all the places I had been showing up as an advisor for divorced women. For example, I was fortunate enough to have been invited by Arianna Huffington to contribute articles to Thrive Global. Luckily, I had full access to my bio and links on my author page. Same with Amazon and other platforms. I simply updated my bio and links to reflect the fact that, while I had assets to support the audience I'd created the material for (for example, the self-led course I'd created), my focus was now on serving entrepreneurs.

So, Google your business. Look at all the places where your business is listed. What needs tweaking? What can you update yourself, and who do you need to contact to facilitate updates? Pay particular attention to listings on sites like Google Reviews, Yelp, TripAdvisor, or any other review site that might have picked up your information. Those are places where thousands of your ideal clients spend time!

Now, to address the (perfectly coiffed and catfish-filtered) elephant in the room: social media. Despite what the marketing gurus will tell you, social media by itself is *not a strong visibility plan.* Even if you have a good following, you will need more than a few posts to drive sales to your business. Many other pieces of your online visibility plan (website, emails, funnels, online courses, etc.) will need to be in place for you to be successful on social channels. To me, social media is for informing my community about what I'm up to and inviting them to explore further—*not* directly selling.

The big potential in social media is customer engagement. On these platforms, you can cultivate two-way conversations with potential buyers in order to humanize your brand, forge deeper connections, and elevate "like, know, and trust" in ways no traditional advertising format can do. Also, according to Sprout Social in 2021, 55 percent of consumers learned about new brands on social platforms. If you're selling products or services, being where your buyers are is super important.

Networking

Building a strong business network—both in person and online—is crucial to the success of your company. Ask those you meet what their biggest challenges are in business and life. Can you help them? Can you introduce them to someone who can?

Also, please don't do networking like I did as a new business owner! I used to show up to networking meetings with a stack of business cards and refuse to leave until every last one of those babies was handed out. It's what I was taught, but it was a turnoff for many people—for good reason. Just like no one wants to get married after a first date, your ideal clients don't want to be sold to without getting to know you first. Go in with no expectations other than to connect with people you may like and respect. Have genuine conversations. Hand out your cards, but only to people with whom you felt a genuine connection.

(And, for the love of God, please don't do this in the online space, either! "Friending" or connecting with someone only to send a DM with your sales pitch five seconds later is not a viable lead generation strategy. It's the business equivalent of an unsolicited dick pic.)

Content Marketing

When it comes to small-budget, big-yield strategies, content marketing takes the cake. However, to get the most out of this pathway, you should be ready to put substantial time and effort into creating readable, relevant content across multiple platforms (or to hire someone if you don't have the bandwidth or skill set).

Content marketing is great for educating, delivering value, and attracting an aligned audience. It's a strategy that centers your customer and their needs, questions, curiosities, and values, and makes them the hero of the story. As Don Miller writes in his book, Building a Story Brand, "When we position our customer as the hero and ourselves as the guide, we will be recognized as a trusted resource to help them overcome their challenges. Positioning the customer as the hero in the story is more than just good manners; it's also good business." If your audience finds value in your content, they will automatically be attracted to discover more about you and your business.

This doesn't mean you can't invite your audience to join a sales conversation, only that the sales conversation is peripheral to the content. When my client Gina and I were working on her content planning, I sent her some topic ideas for her blog that would allow her to not only educate and nurture her audience but also grow her list by making a soft push toward her "9 Tips" opt-in. Once readers had opted in, she would be able to nurture them through email and enroll them into her sales cycle. None of the blogs she wrote were direct sales pitches. However, because the content was so compelling, she began seeing a 20 percent increase in opt-ins per week on her lead magnets. Her email list grew tremendously in the following months.

Start your content marketing efforts by blogging for your own audience and guest blogging on reputable platforms. Next, start pitching articles to online publications and local media outlets. Remember, volume is important, because more content in the right places can give you access to a broader audience—but if the content doesn't add value to the readers, is too salesy, or is sloppily written, it will be a wasted effort and might even work against your brand. If necessary, invest in support to edit and proofread your work.

Finally, don't be afraid to repurpose. It's easy and helps you continue your visibility efforts while saving time. What can you share this week that you wrote a year ago? Can you break an old article up into pieces, add a few sentences here and there, and re-share across multiple platforms? (One note: be sure to check out the guidelines for the platforms you're using before you share the same articles in multiple places. Some outlets may have rules around repurposing content.)

Media

Getting on TV or in a national magazine takes strategy, consistency, and most importantly, relationship building. How do you do that? Social media, of course! Members of the press have Twitter, Instagram, and Facebook accounts just like the rest of us. Some even have their own YouTube channels. You can follow the stories they are doing, then learn about their life by following them and engaging. (Not stalking! I'm talking about genuine engagement.) If you do this correctly, it will be a pleasant surprise when your name appears on an email in their inbox—and when you get to the interview, it will feel like you already know each other.

The most important thing to remember when pitching the media is that it's not about you, your business, or your expertise. It's all about *their audience*. It's their job to serve up content that their viewers, readers, and listeners will benefit from. Sure, your story or journey or experience is just that—yours. Just make sure that the angle you're pitching is about results for their audience.

Another thing I learned quickly (if you can call sixty-eight hours of pitching story ideas to various outlets "quickly") is that there are no dress rehearsals in television and live radio. No one is going to put you on national TV hoping that you'll be a good guest. So, create your own "dress rehearsals" through video, reels, and livestreams. Find ways to prove yourself beforehand so news outlets know you won't freeze in front of the camera.

Lastly, don't quit before you hit gold. After sixty-eight hours of pitching got me nothing, I went in for another round. In hour sixty-nine, I finally got a call … from the booking producer for *Good Morning America*, who said that she loved my recent pitch—and would I like to do a segment with Eckhart Tolle? Over the last year, I've been fortunate enough to be invited to share tips on everything from money to mindset, passion to profits, and relationship advice to divorce tips in the biggest markets out there—New York, Los Angeles, Chicago, and Washington. I've also been featured in stories and interviews in *Parents, People* and *Entrepreneur*. So, if media feels exciting to you, please don't give up before the miracle happens! Plan for a year of pitching and dig in.

Speaking

There is probably no bigger needle-mover in my business than speaking to an aligned audience about a topic I'm passionate about. Speaking is what moved my business from zero to over six figures in less than twelve months, and continues to grow my business into the millions.

You may think that I've always been outgoing, and that speaking on stage came naturally to me. You'd be wrong. For years, I would literally shake, sweat, and panic before each and every podcast interview, radio segment, and Facebook Live. Heck, I'm *still* terrified of being on live TV. But I do it anyway.

Why? Because after my first radio interview, my phone rang. Because after my first twenty-minute talk to a women's group, I booked $36,000 in business in under ten weeks. Because after my first podcast appearance as a guest, my email list grew by 108 people and I booked twenty-one discovery calls.

Speaking—even at a small scale—creates serious visibility. More, it creates serious *credibility*—both during the presentation itself, and later, when you share about your speaking invitations on social media and your website. "Wow, look, she's doing *another* radio spot!"

Events

Events are simpler than ever to organize and create—and, like other forms of speaking, they generally have a high conversion rate. Think virtual events, in-person workshops, webinars, three-day challenges, etc. There are so many cool (and inexpensive) ways to create events these days—why not try it for yourself?

One caveat: filling an event involves filling seats. If you don't already have an audience, this might not be the best strategy for you. Instead, focus on getting in front of other people's audiences and on their stages to build your own.

***

These are just a few pathways to visibility that you can easily work with right now, today. Chances are, you've played with at least a few of them. If you've tried them before and they haven't worked for you, ask yourself, "Was I consistent?" If not, I'd encourage you to try them again—this time with a solid plan in place to support you.

REFERRALS

In the excitement of enrolling new clients and customers, it can be easy to forget about the ones you have. Yet, if harnessed, they can be a powerful force in driving sales to your business. In fact, there are people in my network who have built seven-figure businesses almost exclusively on referrals!

Like everything else, the first step to getting referrals from your existing clients is to ask! Don't be afraid to reach out to let them know what's coming up for you. One of the best questions to start with is, "Do you have anyone in your network who could benefit from this?" Shoutouts, thank you gifts, and referral commissions can also sweeten the deal for everyone.

Referrals can also come from a strong sphere of influence—which takes us back to networking. Remember to build relationships, not just push for sales. This makes it easy for the people in your network to send their people to you with full confidence and trust. Consider creating a formal referral or affiliate program to reward those who support your business. At a minimum, have a formal process to thank people for the referrals they send, even if you don't land the business.

Finally, always get testimonials! If you're great at what you do, your customers will want to rave about you. Consistently ask for reviews and feedback—both written and on video. You'll be surprised how many people are thrilled to share.

Your Visibility Plan

Now that you have an idea of what visibility strategies might work best for you and your business, let's create a plan for you to engage with them.

Look at all the items on the list below. In your journal, jot down all the ones that interest you and that you are already doing or are willing to try.

Speaking/Events/Media	Virtual	Social Media (e.g.)
Podcast appearances Radio interviews TV interviews Hosting an in-person event or workshop	Virtual workshops Livestreaming (your platforms) Livestreaming (other people's platforms) Virtual summits Webinars	Facebook LinkedIn Instagram Instagram stories TikTok YouTube Twitter Other platforms of your choice
Networking	**Referrals**	**Content**
Local chapters Virtual groups Conferences Masterminds	Email campaigns Virtual coffee/tea Affiliate programs Testimonials (video and print)	Blogs Newsletters Article submissions Vlog/video content

Now, ask yourself, "Which of these will be most powerful for me to focus on over the next twelve months?" Choose no more than one item from each category. Why? Because you can't do it all, nor should you try!

Then, break it down to what you will focus on in the next twelve weeks. Create a plan to do one or two things consistently. Bring in your notes from earlier in this chapter about who your ideal clients are, where you can find them, and what problems you can solve for them. How can you reach them most effectively through the visibility pathways you've chosen?

Lastly, jot down some ideas about *how* you will begin. Under each activity you've chosen, brainstorm three to four ideas and a timeline for completing each one. For example:

- *Speaking.* What can you talk about for twenty minutes without any hesitation? Where can you share your message? Who do you know who has a podcast or radio show where you could be a guest? (Hint: Ask them now!) Commit to speaking at least twice per month for the next three months.

- *Media.* Craft an expert intro to present to media outlets. Craft a story/article pitch and send it to ten editors. Write a press release about your upcoming launch. Commit to pitching one story per week for the next three months.

- *Content.* Brainstorm ten content topics that will serve your ideal audience. Outline the next two months of your business newsletter. Commit to doing one Facebook Live or Instagram Reel a day for the next thirty days. (Hint: Do one now about this awesome business book you are reading, and tag me!)

Remember, you don't have to do it all. You just have to do a few things consistently—and by consistently, I mean multiple times over the course of three to six months.

Go Back to your Vision

Once you find the visibility plan that lights you up, it's easy to go all in—to the point where you forget *why* you're going all in in the first place.

So, before you run with your new visibility plan, I want you to ask yourself, "Does what I've outlined actually align with my vision, core values, and goals?"

If you want a quiet life with lots of time for your kids and spouse, and don't want to drop everything at a moment's notice to film a segment, don't rely on a TV media strategy! If, like Angelica from Chapter 3, you hate social media and don't have multiple hours a week to invest in it, don't make that your primary visibility plan. If you love referrals but hate writing blogs, lean into those connections, baby!

Remember, we are not doing this just to create business success. We're doing this to build a life we love. So, if you're feeling any "shoulds" or resistance around your visibility plan, go back to your values, your "why," and your goals. Are the paths you've chosen actually the most aligned? Or is there a better way for you to grow?

You *can* build a visibility plan without hustle or stress. Just lean into the strategies that truly light you up, which fit the time and energy you want to devote to them, and which most closely align with your personal and business goals.

Grow Powers Flow

As you engage with the Grow Pillar, you'll see clearly how it is both fed by and feeds the Vision and Flow Pillars. The more you do this work around visibility, the more your business will flow. When you update your Flow numbers (which you should do quarterly and annually), you will clearly see how your work in the Grow Pillar has changed your bottom line—and how it's bringing you closer to your Vision every single day.

Now that you know what to do, it's time to work on your Grow mindset and action plan so you can launch into the next stage of creating your dream.

CHAPTER 9

Your Path to Profits

"WHAT A RUSH!" my assistant exclaimed. "More than 260 connections made. That's so exciting!"

"It sure is," I replied.

We had just closed out our most recent virtual "speed networking" event which brought together our EnVision + Thrive Academy members and our greater community to make new connections and foster collaboration. It certainly felt like our intentions had been realized!

I dreamed up the EnVision + Thrive Academy on March 16, 2020. Lockdowns had just been announced, and businesses all across America were being forced to close their doors. I knew the fallout would be huge, especially since so many businesses—particularly those in the first three to five years of operation—were already financially insecure. In the first forty-eight hours of the shutdowns, I spent twenty hours putting out content to guide entrepreneurs on their next steps—like calling all their vendors and creditors to discuss putting "holds" on upcoming payments that they would now be unable to make and asking for freezes on future payments for at least ninety days. I knew the importance of these financial triage steps because for years I'd been advising clients after fires, floods, and other catastrophic losses to their businesses and revenues.

My phone rang constantly during those first few weeks. Everyone needed support—but I was already full with one-on-one clients and didn't have the bandwidth to add more. However, I knew I needed to be part of the solution, and through a community model I could support many more entrepreneurs than I could with private coaching and events alone. I could bring my own knowledge and that of other experts to the table to lead entrepreneurs through one of the hardest times they, and their businesses, might ever need to endure.

Creating the Academy felt aligned not only because I was responding to a clear need, but because I was responding to that need in a way that honored my values, my "why," and my goals. I structured this offer in a way that could help my clients thrive through a massive challenge but also wouldn't burn me out. I worked within my Vision, Flow, and Grow Pillars to get clear on what was, and was not, aligned for me to do at this time. The entire creation and launch process felt easy, natural, and exciting—just as I had EnVisioned it.

Start the Engine

Woo-hoo! You made it! You've come through the EnVision process to plan your Path to Profits. You may feel a bit like you're taxiing on the runway, getting ready to take to the skies!

This chapter is all about takeoff. We're going to gather everything you've learned and created over the course of this book and drop it into an action plan that will launch you to 37,000 feet. More, we're going to check in on the mindset pieces that will make a smooth ascent not only possible, but fun.

Here are the pieces of the action plan we'll be fleshing out over the next several pages:

- Your new routines and habits
- Your next bold moves
- Your support structure

YOUR NEW ROUTINES AND HABITS

If you want different results, do different things.

It sounds so simple. And yet, the things we do every day without thinking are not always calculated to support our success. So, as you get ready for takeoff, grab your journal and ask yourself:

- "What do I need to do differently to create the success I desire?"
- "What new routines are required for my goals to come to fruition?"

- "What can I no longer afford to do?"
- "Where do I need help?"

Write down everything that comes to mind. Dig deep and get the answers you need. Remember, stay centered here, and be careful not to confuse success with happiness.

When you're done, jot down the ways you might implement the changes required (action steps). Try to come up with more than one action step for each answer—if you keep digging, you'll get more creative! Don't forget to add the financial costs of implementing these new routines and habits to your Guidepost #5 financial goal!

Here are some examples of how this might look:

"What do I need to do differently to succeed?"

- *I need to get better sleep*
  - Go to bed half an hour earlier
  - Turn off my phone at 9:00 p.m.
  - Don't eat dinner after 7:00 p.m.
  - Get a monthly massage ($150/month)

- *I need to manage my stress*
  - Take a long walk three times a week
  - Order new vitamins/supplements ($30/month)
  - Take a breathwork class twice a week ($100/month)

- *I need to focus on one thing at a time*
  - Download a focus timer app
  - Revamp my calendar using a time-blocking system
  - Silence/remove notifications on my phone

"What new routines are required for my goals to come to fruition?"

- *I will eat at regular times to help me meet my health goals*
  - Do meal prep on weekends
  - Set a calendar alert for mealtimes
  - Order pre-prepared meals from my local caterer ($200/week)

- *I will make three connection calls per day*
  - Download and use a robust CRM (Customer Relationship Management) program ($15/month)
  - Keep a running list in my phone of people I would like to reach out to
  - Block time in my calendar for making calls

"What can I no longer afford to do?"

- *I can no longer afford to waste fifteen hours a month on bookkeeping tasks*
  - Hire a bookkeeper ($250/month)
  - Upgrade my bookkeeping software ($50/month)
  - Invest in an online course or product to simplify the process ($499)

- *I can no longer afford to hide during networking events*
  - Commit to having at least three conversations at every event
  - Ask to speak at an upcoming event
  - Purchase an outfit that makes you feel confident and assertive ($250)

- *If I want to reach my big goals, I can no longer afford to overspend my personal budget*
  - Carry cash so that I can only spend what I have allotted for this week/month
  - Reduce takeout purchases from four nights per week to two

"Where do I need help?"

- *I need help managing my onboarding process so I can focus on sales*
  - Hire a part-time business manager ($1,000+/ month)
  - Purchase robust project management software to streamline your organizational flow, and pay someone to set it up

- *I need help staying accountable to my big vision*
  - Join a mastermind in your industry (Free to $50,000 or more per year)
  - Hire a qualified business advisor ($10,000 to $100,000+ per year)
  - Create a peer group with other business owners. Meet once a month to keep each other motivated and cheer each other on.

YOUR NEXT BOLD MOVES

Sometimes, it only takes one bold move to set massive change into motion!

What three actions will you take in the next thirty days to

create immediate and positive change in your life and business? What one action will you take in the next seven days?

These could be actions you already identified as part of your visibility strategy in Chapter 8, or they could be something you want to do for yourself personally. Either way, write your bold actions out on paper with deadlines alongside. Post them where you can see them every day. And don't forget to celebrate yourself when you complete them!

YOUR SUPPORT STRUCTURE

Remember, you can't *have* it all if you're trying to *do* it all. Chances are, there are people all around you that would be thrilled to help you take the leap to the next level in your life and business.

So, ask yourself, "Who will I call when I need …?"

- High-level business networking/introductions
- Mentoring and inspiration
- Financial/tax/investment planning and support
- Bookkeeping/financial strategy support
- Marketing support
- Childcare or family support
- Health and wellness support
- Emotional support/therapy
- Spiritual support
- A shoulder to cry on
- An objective perspective
- A swift kick in the pants

Make a physical list that includes the names of these individuals, their phone numbers, and their email addresses. Keep it in your desk drawer or pin it to your wall. That way, when you're having a challenge, you don't need to think about who to call—you will already know!

Onward and Upward

Flowing and Growing into your Vision is an ongoing process. Inside my EnVision + Thrive Academy I continually advise members to do the following things:

Daily

Revisit the Vision Statement you created in Chapter 2. I suggest reading it out loud as part of your morning routine. Look at and review your vision board.

Weekly

What gets scheduled gets done.

Look at your calendar for the upcoming week, and then look at your goals list. Are there clear tasks in support of your goal on your agenda? Or is your week filled with busy work, unnecessary meetings, or other nonessential tasks? If at least three actions toward your one-year goals aren't on your calendar each and every week, add them in now.

Sharing your plans with others who are on the Path to Profits adds an element of accountability. I currently ask for weekly check-ins inside the EnVision + Thrive Academy on Fridays and Sundays—Fridays for weekly wins, and Sundays for choosing action steps for the upcoming week. I love the culture of collaboration this creates. And when someone hits a big goal, we *all* celebrate.

Quarterly

If you haven't broken down your big vision into years, and from there into quarters, it can be a lot harder to hit the mark. I love to sit down two weeks in advance of the new quarter and put my "momentum plans" into play. I look at the twelve weeks ahead and mark off holidays, travel days, time with family, speaking engagements, etc. Then, I add action steps aligned with my goals, along with benchmarks and deadlines for the projects I will initiate or continue in the coming quarter.

Again, make sure that the things you're choosing to spend your time and resources on are aligned with your core values, your "why," and your goals—not what you think "has to" be done in your business!

What if You Don't?

"What if you don't actually do *any* of this?"

When I ask this question at my EnVision events, the room goes silent. No one wants to consider what it means to do nothing—and yet, despite all the amazing information and support available for them, this is precisely what some entrepreneurs will do.

Maybe it feels like too much work to engage with the Vision, Flow, and Grow Pillars in a meaningful way. Maybe it feels too overwhelming to actually look at what's happening. Maybe they know if they do this work, they will have to make the big changes they've been avoiding for months or years. Maybe they just don't have the drive to do better.

Maybe some of those feel true for you, too. Maybe you're thinking, "It would be great if I actually had the bandwidth to implement everything in this book, but I don't. I have more important things to concentrate on."

I get it. And that's totally your call. Free will is a real thing. But before you make a free-will decision, you should understand the choice you're *actually* making.

There is a cost to doing nothing, just like there is a cost to evolving—and a small shift now can make all the difference later. For example, if an airplane is taking off from Los Angeles for Boston, but you point its nose five degrees south as it ascends, it will end up somewhere in the Carolinas—nearly a thousand miles from its intended destination. In the same way, ignoring this work may not feel detrimental today, or tomorrow—but in the long term, the cost of doing nothing could be very high indeed. It might be purely monetary—those fun family vacations, that new car, that bigger house. Or it might be to your quality of life, missed opportunities, or time with those you love.

And, if you continue to do nothing, the cost might be your dream life. Your family legacy. The full expression of your purpose.

So, go ahead and ask yourself, "What if I don't?" Follow that five-degree shift to its conclusion. And then, use what you are shown to feed your "why."

I believe in you. I know you can do this work, even if it feels hard and confronting. I know you can do it because your business is worth it. Your vision is worth it. *You* are worth it.

Afterword

IT'S 6:30 A.M. and I'm sitting on the steps of the LaPlaya Beach Resort in Naples, Florida. As I wait for the sunrise, the birds are singing loudly. The waves are kissing the shore with rhythmic grace. The sky seems vastly wider, full of possibility. I feel a blend of peaceful calm and overwhelming excitement for what is coming. Tears flood my eyes as I take in the beauty of this morning, the promise of the day.

I am grateful beyond measure.

There's something surreal about knowing you are sitting in your grandest vision—that you are exactly where you are supposed to be in this moment, and that everything in your life is fully in support of you. This morning, I have stepped out of the hustle, the grind, even time itself. What I desire is no longer "out there"; it's right here, right now.

If you asked me ten years ago if I thought I would (or could) be here, in this beautiful location, doing a site visit for one of my signature EnVision retreats, I would have said, "Hell, no. I don't have time for that!" I would have pegged this as a vacation spot for sure, a place to come to nurse my ever-present work hangover and set aside the CEO mask for a while. But to be here, planning a retreat to bring other leading entrepreneurs together in community and create space to mentor their dreams? Not a chance.

Three years ago, though, I would have jumped for joy at the prospect, even if I had no idea yet how I would make it happen. In fact, Naples featured prominently on my vision boards for years.

That's the thing about vision.

Sometimes, we find ourselves on dark roads. We can't see more than a few feet in front of us; we just know we have to keep our heads down and keep moving. But when we have clarity about what we want—better yet, when we have a proven system to create that clarity—it's like switching on the high beams. We can see further, wider, and in more detail than ever before. Suddenly, we know where to turn, where to swerve, and when to hit the gas, baby. We can see our way to our destination, and make better choices about how to get there as quickly as possible, with fewer distractions.

That's what the EnVision process is all about.

You now have all the tools you require to create your dream life and the business to support it. You've learned how to leverage your values and your "why" to set aligned goals. You've bravely faced down the monster under your bed (aka, your business numbers), and created a plan to bridge the gap from where you are to where you want to be.

You are closer than ever to creating your dream. It's right on the horizon. And you will get there—because now you know the way.

As you explore new ways of growing profits, you will likely learn about the growing popularity of purpose-driven businesses—also referred to as "conscious capitalism." This holistic approach provides not only financial wealth to stakeholders, but also intellectual, cultural, ecological, emotional, and social wealth to business owners, employees, and customers. Conscious capitalists consider their impact on the planet and their local neighborhood, as well as the impact on their bottom line.

If you're not already thinking along these lines, I encourage you to start. After all, through the work you've done in this book, you've broken through into a new paradigm: "I can have it all." Conscious capitalism invites an even juicer reality: "We can have it all."

So please, even if your business isn't quite where you'd like it to be today, keep going. Do it for yourself—for your dreams, your legacy, and your contribution to the world. Do it for those who will come after you, and who will look to you as an example of how to thrive in business. And do it for the world, because the world needs *you*.

Yours in abundance, now and always,

Michelle

Leave a Review

Spread the love!

Scan the QR code below to leave a review on the site where
you purchased this book. Your feedback will help other
entrepreneurs find this work, too!

Resources

Download your Flow Pillar spreadsheets and other
supportive resources for the EnVision process
www.michellejacobik.com/pathtoprofitsresources

Book Michelle to speak at your next conference or event
Email: info@michellejacobik.com

Discover the EnVision + Thrive Academy
www.bit.ly/JoinEnVisionThriveAcademy

Connect with us on social media

 www.instagram.com/michellejacobik

 www.facebook.com/michellejacobik

vm.tiktok.com/ZTRL4GK7c

 www.linkedin.com/in/michelle-jacobik-267724

Grab Michelle's EnVision Oracle Card Deck
www.amzn.to/3Hdl2Vc

Acknowledgments

TO EVERY ENTREPRENEUR who has ignited their dreams of business ownership and invited me onto their path: The journey with each of you has been heart-driven, purposeful, and downright fabulous. Thank you for letting me be part of your board of advisors, and for trusting me not only with your dollars and cents but with protecting and growing your "baby" and your prosperity dreams.

To Jody, my husband, my best friend and biggest cheerleader: You have been not only my rock, but also my inspiration and example to become the best version of myself. You are a constant reminder that dreams do come true. You have continually walked with me, allowing my prosperity journey to unfold alongside of yours, encouraging me with love and appreciation. I adore you and love you beyond words!

To my children, Alex and Amanda, and my stepsons, Brandon, Chase, and Calvin: Thank you for embracing and rising through the storms that were not of your choosing, and for trusting me when all I could muster was a promise to provide you a safe and loving home and a listening ear. Thank you for all your sacrifices in those early years, and for having "listening ears" as we dialed up Rich Dad Poor Dad, Tony Robbins, Wayne Dyer, Gary Vee, Ed Mylett, and other inspirational voices on our car rides. I love our exchanges of motivational content and I've learned more from your shares than you know. Your kindness, passion, work ethic, and entrepreneurial spirit make me beam with pride. As I watch you all spread your own wings, building businesses and lives of your own, I see the results of all those times we said, "I'll pay for what you need, not for what you want." You no longer ask, "Can I have it?" but instead, "How can I create it?" Keep EnVisioning, reaching for the stars, and building lives you love!

To Dan and Heather, my manifesting dream team: I will forever be grateful for our friendship and for the sacred space you offered me to activate the creative juices to write the majority of this book. Your offer came at the exact time when I needed support the most. I'm so excited about the parallels of this next chapter we are all about to embark on, and I'm looking forward to building many new memories with you both. Let's keep ordering it up!

To my brother, Norman: Whenever I feel lost or stuck in this lifetime, you always seem to have your finger on the "high beam" switch. You show me again and again that my path is lit, that I wasn't lost after all, and that there are clear next steps.

I'll never take your undying love and supportive shoulder for granted. You are a gift!

To Bryna Haynes, my editor and creative partner in crime: Thank you for taking this project and for creating some real Thelma and Louise-style fun between us. Thank you for the day in Naples, where I first got this book out of my head and heart and put voice to it. Thank you for your patience with me as I pivoted from doing this work early last year into doing it in the perfect time; it was after that visit to Naples that I decided to make a big, unplanned geographical change that aligned with me stepping into my biggest vision for my life. Your mission and vision to bring conscious leadership and purposeful creative works into the world is vast and inspires me beyond what you can imagine. To know that I will be among the ranks of the published authors at WorldChangers Media is an honor. Thank you for your willingness to work during the wee hours of the night over these past few months, while everyone else was sleeping, to make my project come to life. You are a rockstar!

To Esther Hicks, Boni Lonnsburry, Cheryl Richardson, and so many other women trailblazing the way in front of me: Ysou remind me daily through your writings and teachings to create consciously on my own path of least resistance, and to trust the journey. I'm in the most trusting spaces of life these last five years, and it feels so, so good!

About the Author

MICHELLE JACOBIK is a highly sought-after Business Profitability Strategist and Success Coach who helps highly-motivated entrepreneurs understand their unique potential so they can achieve their big goals in less time and with more ease.

She is an expert at helping business owners master their vision, mindset, money and business growth. In addition to her education in insurance and finance, she transformed her own life as a twenty-three-year-old young woman, drowning in a sea of debt, to a businesswoman who, with her partner, bought the company they worked for (at the age of twenty-nine), and grew that client base from $600,000 to over $12 million in sales a year.

Today she transfers her experience and insights as a seasoned entrepreneur and mentor, sharing her powerful strategies, and has built a successful coaching practice while traveling the country doing what she loves.

Clients refer to Michelle as "an inspiring, fierce leader," "a compassionate professional with passion, drive, and seemingly infinite positivity," and "an incredibly powerful coach with the skill to deliver what is most needed with precision ... all fueled by a desire to see others create lives and businesses that fully serve them and their vision." She speaks across the country, delivering messages of financial empowerment to her audiences, and has appeared on various popular media outlets, including ABC, CBS, FOX, PIX11 NYC, Parents, People, Entrepreneur, and Thrive Global.

Michelle lives with her husband, Jody, in Naples, Florida. Learn more about her work at www.MichelleJacobik.com.

About the Publisher

FOUNDED IN 2021 by Bryna Haynes, WorldChangers Media is a boutique publishing company focused on "Ideas for Impact." We know that great books change lives, topple outdated paradigms, and build movements. Our commitment is to deliver superior-quality transformational nonfiction by, and for, the next generation of thought leaders.

Ready to write and publish your thought leadership book with us? Learn more at www.WorldChangers.Media.

Made in the USA
Middletown, DE
06 October 2022

11939081R00118